THE
STUDENT LOAN
HANDBOOK
FOR LAW STUDENTS
AND ATTORNEYS

ADAM S. MINSKY

ABA**LAW**
PRACTICE
DIVISION
The Business of Practicing Law

Commitment to Quality: The Law Practice Division is committed to quality in our publications. Our authors are experienced practitioners in their fields. Prior to publication, the contents of all our books are rigorously reviewed by experts to ensure the highest quality product and presentation. Because we are committed to serving our readers' needs, we welcome your feedback on how we can improve future editions of this book.

Cover design by Andrew Alcala/ABA Publishing

Printed in the United States of America.

20 19 18 17 16   5 4 3 2 1

Library of Congress Cataloging-in-Publication Data
Names: Minsky, Adam S., author.
Title: The student loan handbook for law students and attorneys / Adam S. Minsky.
Description: Chicago : American Bar Association, 2016. | Includes index.
Identifiers: LCCN 2015048057 (print) | LCCN 2015048203 (ebook) | ISBN 9781634254434 (softcover : alk. paper) | ISBN 9781634254441 ()
Subjects: LCSH: Student aid--Law and legislation--United States. | Student loans--United States.
Classification: LCC KF4235 .M565 2016 (print) | LCC KF4235 (ebook) | DDC 378.3/620973--dc23
LC record available at http://lccn.loc.gov/2015048057

Discounts are available for books ordered in bulk. Special consideration is given to state bars, CLE programs, and other bar-related organizations. Inquire at Book Publishing, American Bar Association, 321 N. Clark Street, Chicago, Illinois 60654.

www.ShopABA.org

For Joshua

Disclaimer

I'm an attorney, and I wouldn't be a true attorney if I didn't start this off with some important disclaimers:

This book is not an advertisement.

The material contained in this book is for informational purposes only and does not constitute legal advice. Reading this book is not a substitute for obtaining legal advice from an attorney.

Reading this book does not create an attorney-client relationship. This book is not intended to create, and does not constitute, a contract for representation by Adam S. Minsky, Esq.

The laws governing student loans are constantly changing, so I cannot guarantee that the material or information contained in this book is correct, complete, or up-to-date at the time you read it.

There. Don't we all feel better now?

Table of Contents

PART 1

A Crash Course in
Student Loans

1

Introduction

In 2013, student loan debt in the United States surpassed $1 trillion. That's more than credit card debt or automobile debt—and it's growing faster than any other type of consumer debt.

According to the Institute for College Access and Success, the average undergraduate student at a nonprofit state college or university took on nearly $30,000 in student loan debt in 2012.[1] That's up from $18,750 in 2004, an increase of more than 56 percent over the course of eight years. In 2012, 71 percent of college students graduated with student loan debt, up from 65 percent in 2004. And that's just undergraduate students.

When you throw law graduates into the mix, the numbers are even more staggering. According to Law School Transparency, nearly 85 percent of law school graduates take out student loans to fund their legal education.[2] Law students graduating in 2010 had an average law school debt burden of $77,634 at public law schools and $112,007 at private law schools. Furthermore, according to the American Bar Association, in 2012 the average student debt load for public law school graduates was $84,600, and for private law school graduates it was $112,158. To be clear, that's just law school debt, and that's just the averages. Because many students who borrow for law school also took out loans to fund their undergraduate education, it's painfully obvious that law students from both public and private law schools are easily graduating with debt burdens exceeding $100,000—and it's often much more. In the country with the highest levels of student loan debt in the world, law school graduates have some of the worst debt burdens.

Graduating with such extreme levels of student loan debt would be problematic and overwhelming for anyone, but law graduates face unique challenges because of their wildly varied career paths and associated incomes. The public defender or assistant district attorney may start out making less than $50,000 per year. Here in Massachusetts where I practice, their salaries can be below $40,000. Repaying $100,000 in student loans on that salary may seem impossible. The big firm associate or corporate attorney may have a six-figure salary, but he or she will face a different set of challenges and choices in terms of the optimal repayment approach. Meanwhile, small-firm associates, solo practitioners, and contract attorneys will

---

1 *See* The Institute for College Access and Success, Project on Student Debt, available at: http://ticas.org/posd/home
2 *See* Law School Transparency, available at: http://www.lawschooltransparency.com/

encounter their own student loan repayment problems, given the inherent fluctuations and unpredictability of their income.

I've been helping student loan borrowers for several years in my law practice, and I know that there are minimal resources to help people manage their student debt. It's incredibly easy to *get* student loans—financial aid award packages are neatly organized for you in a professional letter, and all you have to do is fill out some paperwork and sign on the dotted line—but when you leave your educational institution and you're stuck with all that debt, understanding your options and creating a plan can be a mind-boggling undertaking, especially when you're already struggling with tasks like finding a job, studying for the bar exam, or adjusting to a new home or work environment. To make things worse, many student loan servicing companies are bureaucratic behemoths, too large and disorganized to provide the customer service that borrowers need. It can be completely overwhelming to get any straight answers, and too often I see student borrowers—especially attorneys—get into big trouble with their loans simply because they did not understand their rights and options.

There are a lot of books about "tricks" or "secrets" for getting rid of your student loan debt entirely. Sadly, these books are usually filled with bad advice, playing on graduates' desperation to climb out from under their massive debt. This book is based on a hard but important truth: your student loans are probably here to stay, at least for a while, and your best bet is to understand your options so that you can keep them in good standing, avoid nasty consequences, and make progress toward loan freedom (whether that's by paying everything off in full or by getting on track for loan forgiveness programs).

I've designed this handbook to be a concise, easy-to-read guide to help you understand your student loans, how they work, and how you can manage them effectively as a law student and as an attorney. Part 1 is applicable to everyone, whereas Part 2 examines the options available to attorneys in specific career paths. This is not legalese, and this is not a legal practice manual. This is a guidebook. Everyone's situation is different, and everyone's needs are unique, but I hope this book can be a starting point for law students and attorneys who have student loan debt. If you get started down the right path at the beginning, it will just make your life easier.

There is no magic bullet, no button you can press or secret application to make your student loans disappear with the snap of your fingers. But, when armed with solid facts and sound strategies, you can manage your loans effectively and focus on the more enjoyable parts of your life.

With this in mind, let's get started.

2

Student Loan Types

The first step in trying to understand your student loans—and your options—is getting to know the different *types* of student loans. There are essentially two types of student loans: federal student loans and private student loans.

✳   *Federal loans* are either lent directly, or backed (guaranteed) by the federal government. Federal lenders provide many options to borrowers that allow for repayment flexibility and loan management. Interest rates also tend to be lower than for private loans.

✳   *Private loans* are made by private entities and are not backed by the federal government. Private student loans can be originated by a bank, a commercial lender (such as Sallie Mae), a nonprofit organization, or a state agency. The options available for federal student loans are generally not available for private student loans, which can make managing private loans a lot more difficult.

> **TIP**   Don't know whether your student loans are federal or private? The National Student Loan Data System (NSLDS), available at www.nslds.ed.gov, is a database that lists all of the federal student loans that you have ever received. This is a unique database that lists all of *your specific* federal student loans. If you have a student loan that is not listed on the database, it is probably private.

There are fundamental differences between federal and private student loans. On the one hand, federal lenders provide many options that can be very helpful in managing repayment. These options include federal loan consolidation, a menu of repayment plan options (including plans that can be tied to your income), generous *deferment* and *forbearance* options that allow you to postpone your payments under certain circumstances, and the possibility of loan forgiveness.

Unfortunately, these options are generally not available for private student loans. Typically, private student loans have fewer repayment plans, stricter loan terms, higher interest rates, and less generous options if you ever find yourself in a financial bind.

On the other hand, when you default on federal student loans, the consequences can be much more severe, because the federal government has extraordinarily powerful collection tools to pursue defaulted borrowers. There's no statute of limitations on federal student loans, meaning that the federal government can literally pursue

✳ Statute of limitation on private loans?

you to the grave. So be careful, and avoid default. We'll talk more about default later.

Federal student loans come in two broad varieties: "guaranteed" federal loans through the "FFEL" program and "Direct" federal loans issued directly by the U.S. Department of Education.

Federal Family Education Loan (FFEL) Program

Until 2010, many federal student loans were issued via the Federal Family Education Loan (FFEL) program, under which banks or other private lenders issued federally guaranteed loans. The program was eliminated in 2010, so if you took out all of your federal loans after that, you can skip ahead to the "Direct Federal Loans" section. But if you took out student loans during or prior to 2010, you may have FFEL loans. The FFEL program works like this:

A private entity (such as a bank or other commercial lending institution, like Sallie Mae) lent you the money that helped you pay for school. This was your FFEL lender. As long as you remain in good standing on your loan, your FFEL lender probably doesn't change. The only exception is if your lender sells your loan to a new FFEL lender, which does happen from time to time.

The loan is "guaranteed," or "backed," by a state agency or state-established nonprofit organization, called a **guarantor** or **guaranty agency**. If you ever default on that loan, the guarantor pays the FFEL lender for the remaining balance of your defaulted loan and takes it over. You, in turn, now owe the guarantor rather than the original lender.

However, the chain doesn't end there. Guarantors are ultimately insured by the federal government. If the guaranty agency fails to resolve the default adequately, it can assign the loan to the U.S. Department of Education for collection.

Although FFEL lenders are private, these loans are considered federal because the federal government guarantees them. The loan program is also governed by federal law, and the contracts are issued pursuant to federal regulations.

If this system sounds convoluted to you, welcome to the club. FFEL loans could be quite lucrative for private lenders because they could charge high interest rates and were essentially *guaranteed* full repayment in the event that the borrower defaulted. These were no-risk loans for lenders, even though they were immensely confusing to borrowers. Borrower confusion is one of the reasons why the program was discontinued in 2010. Still, there are millions of borrowers out there who have FFEL loans. This matters, because FFEL program loans are not eligible for all of the federal repayment assistance programs currently available to borrowers. But don't panic if you have FFEL loans—this is fixable (more on that later).

Direct Federal Loans

Most federal student loans issued since 2010, and some loans issued before then as well, are Direct federal loans. These loans are issued directly by the U.S. Department of Education. There are no private lenders or guaranty agencies involved. Regardless of whether the loan is in default or good standing, you will always just owe the U.S. Department of Education. Simple, right? Not so fast.

 Day-to-day billing operations for Direct loans are handled by private **loan servicing companies** contracted by the U.S. Department of Education. In other words, even though your money ultimately goes to the U.S. Department of Education, you actually make payments to the private loan servicer. There are many different loan servicers, but most borrowers who have Direct federal loans will be serviced by one of four major loan servicing companies: Navient (formerly Sallie Mae), NelNet, FedLoan Servicing/PHEAA, or Great Lakes Higher Education.

 TIP If you're not sure whether your federal loans are FFEL or Direct, you can check the National Student Loan Data System (NSLDS) (available at www.nslds.ed.gov). Direct loans will be listed as "Direct" in the database. FFEL loans will either be listed as "FFEL" or will not have the word "Direct" in front of the loan name (for example, a "Direct Stafford Loan" vs. a "Stafford Loan"). If you click on an individual loan, the database will also identify your current loan servicer.

There are several different subtypes of federal student loans, and some are better than others. Except for Perkins loans (discussed first in the following subsections), these federal loans can either be "FFEL" or "Direct" program loans, depending on when you obtained the loan and who your federal lender is.

Federal Perkins Loans

These are neither FFEL nor "Direct" loans; rather, these are low-interest federal student loans that are issued directly by your educational institution. They are available to both undergraduate and graduate students who have significant financial need. Perkins loans have low, fixed interest rates of 5 percent and small disbursement balances. Also, interest does not accrue while you are enrolled in school, and they have fairly generous forgiveness and cancellation options if you work in certain professions.

Federal Subsidized Stafford Loans

Federal subsidized Stafford loans are the most common student loans. They used to be available to undergraduate, graduate, and professional students, but since

2012 they are available only to undergraduate students. If you took out student loans for college, or if you were in law school prior to 2012, you may have subsidized Stafford loans. Otherwise, your law school Stafford loans are unsubsidized (discussed later). The "subsidy" means that the government pays your interest during school enrollment and other qualifying deferment periods, which is a huge benefit of this type of loan.

Federal Unsubsidized Stafford Loans *No!*

Unsubsidized Stafford loans are the subsidized Stafford loan's evil twin. Although they tend to have relatively low interest rates, they are typically disbursed with larger balances. They can be especially costly for students because the government does not cover interest during school or other deferment periods. As soon as you take out that unsubsidized federal Stafford loan during your first year of law school, it starts accruing interest, and that won't stop. Starting in 2012, the only Stafford loans available to graduate and professional students, including law students, are this unsubsidized variety, due to federal budgetary changes made by Congress.   *↑ capped annually?*

Federal Graduate PLUS Loans

Graduate PLUS loans are available only to graduate and professional students, not undergraduates. They have much higher interest rates than other federal student loans and they may also have somewhat high **origination fees**, which are fees tacked on to the initial loan balance to cover administrative costs. Students can borrow up to the cost of attendance, but the loans are not subsidized. Large balances, high interest rates, and the lack of subsidies make these loans extremely costly, particularly for graduate and professional students who may be enrolled in their programs for several years. Because Stafford loan disbursements are capped annually, and Graduate PLUS loans are capped only by the total cost of attendance at your educational institution, many law students rely heavily on Graduate PLUS loans to finance their legal education.   *↑ capped only by the total cost of attendance*

Federal Parent PLUS Loans *No!*

Federal Parent PLUS loans are, in my opinion, the worst federal student loans. These loans are issued to *parents* for the benefit of their child's education, so the parent (not the student) is the borrower and the one who is legally responsible for the debt. Like Graduate PLUS loans, Parent PLUS loans have high balance limits, high interest rates, and origination fees, and they are not subsidized. To make matters even worse, in most cases they are not eligible for income-driven repayment plans.

Summary Chart of Federal Student Loan Types

	Borrower	Interest Rates	Interest Details	Origination Fees	Max Balance Limit
Federal Perkins Loans	Graduate and undergraduate students	Low (5%)	Does not accrue during school	None	Small (under $10,000)
Federal Subsidized Stafford Loans	**Before 2012** Graduate and undergraduate students **Since 2012** Undergraduate students only	Moderate (4.3% to 8.25%)	Paid by government during school	Low (1–2%)	Moderate ($10,000 to $20,000)
Federal Unsubsidized Stafford Loans	Student	Moderate (5.8% to 9.5%)	Begins accruing immediately	Low (1–2%)	Moderate ($10,000 to $20,000)
Federal Graduate PLUS Loans	Student	High (6.8% to 9.5%)	Begins accruing immediately	High (4–5%)	Large (over $20,000)
Federal Parent PLUS Loans	Parent	High (6.8% to 10.5%)	Begins accruing immediately	High (4–5%)	Large (over $20,000)

Private Student Loans

To put it simply, private student loans are any type of educational debt that is *not* originated directly or "backed" by the federal government. Private loans are usually issued by banks or other commercial lenders. Certain states also have state-based student lending programs, and some educational institutions issue private student loans themselves. Although the terms and conditions of these loans differ depending on the specific lender and loan program, they are all nonfederal and, therefore, "private" in nature.

There are some benefits to private student loans. They are easier to obtain. You may not have to worry about college financial aid application cycles or filling out the Free Application for Federal Student Aid (aka the "FAFSA" form). Private loans may offer greater flexibility to shop around for a lower interest rate. Private loans also can be available to borrowers for programs that may not be eligible for federal financial assistance. For instance, many law students take on private *bar study loans* to cover living expenses and training courses during the post-graduation bar examination period; since you are no longer "in school" at this point, you would not be eligible for any more federal financial aid, so a private bar study loan can be an attractive option for many people.

However, private student loans don't have the same built-in rights and protections that federal student loans have. There are usually fewer repayment plan options, and those that are available are less favorable. Consolidation options are severely limited, so you may be stuck paying multiple private loan lenders and servicers. We will cover consolidation later.

Depending on the loan terms, a private lender may have broad discretion to decide whether you can postpone your payments during difficult economic times. In recent years, lenders have increasingly been opting to default unpaid student loans and send them to collection agencies, rather than grant extended deferments, modify the loan repayment terms, or otherwise work with distressed borrowers.

 TIP Contact your private loan lender or servicer to find out your repayment or deferment options.

For these reasons, I generally recommend that students steer clear of private student loans whenever possible. Unless we see nationwide student loan reform that specifically includes private student loans, these types of loans will continue to be restrictive, risky, and in some cases, predatory. Stick to federal student loans if you can. If you must take out private student loans, know that they come with fewer rights and potentially greater risks.

Private Student Loan Quirks

In addition to their inherent restrictiveness, private student loans are distinct from their federal counterparts in several ways.

Cosigners. Many private student loan lenders require, or strongly encourage, the student borrower to obtain a *cosigner*: someone who signs the loan contract right along with the student borrower. Student loan borrowers generally need cosigners for a few reasons:

- Student borrowers may not have good enough credit history to obtain a loan on their own. This is relevant for undergraduate borrowers who may have no credit history at all, or those who have had trouble making payments on other debts in the past.
- The private lender may offer a substantially lower interest rate for a cosigned loan, as compared to a loan that is signed by the student alone.
- The private lender may just require a cosigner, period, as a matter of policy.

Statistics on private student loans are difficult to come by. But as a student loan attorney, I can tell you that the majority of private loan cases that come through my office have a cosigner. Private student loans that have a single signature (the student borrower) tend to be rather rare, at least for loans that get into trouble. In contrast, most federal student loans do not require or even allow a cosigner (the exception is a small number of Parent PLUS loans).

There's a basic rule for cosigners that many people just do not fully understand or appreciate: **The cosigner is *fully* legally responsible for the entire student loan, just as the borrower is.**

This can be problematic if the borrower falls behind on the cosigned private student loans. The cosigner is usually a well-meaning parent, spouse, boyfriend, girlfriend, cousin, or friend. She is helping the borrower go to school to get an education. All the cosigner is doing, says the conventional wisdom, is enabling the student to get that loan that will pay for tuition so that the student can get that degree, get that good job, and get ahead in life. And the student will, of course, get employed upon graduation and promises (promises!) to pay the loan back. The cosigner won't even have to think about it.

The problem is that it doesn't always work that way. And, because the cosigner is fully legally responsible for the loan just as the borrower is, if the student borrower doesn't pay the bill, the cosigner has to do it. I've seen this happen for all sorts of reasons, such as:

- The student doesn't get a high-paying dream job after graduating (or worse, remains unemployed).
- The student gets injured and needs to make medical payments.
- The student simply doesn't understand the consequences of default and chooses to spend money on other things.

In these cases, the lender will pursue both the borrower and the cosigner. The lender will not care that you cosigned that loan for your college boyfriend 10 years ago and have long since broken up—you are still legally responsible for the loan if he stops making payments. Cosigning is a very nasty business. If no payments are made by the borrower or cosigner, the loan is put into default. This means that the cosigner defaults on the loan, too, and she or he will get to experience the joys of debt collection and negative credit consequences right along with the borrower.

Cosigner Release. Luckily, there may be a way out for the cosigner. Some private lenders allow something called a *cosigner release*, whereby the lender lets the cosigner off the hook under certain conditions. These conditions vary from lender to lender, and the specifics may be outlined in the loan's original promissory note. In my experience, they come in two forms:

1. *Buyout*: a single lump-sum payment by the cosigner.
2. *Temporary installment arrangement*: a series of on-time monthly payments by the cosigner over the course of 12 to 48 months (depending on the lender and the loan terms).

In some cases, you can get a cosigner release only while the borrower is making regular payments (before the loan runs into any problems). Other lenders allow a cosigner release even if the cosigner is the one making loan payments. If the conditions are met, the cosigner *may*, at the discretion of the lender, be released from all legal responsibility on the loan, leaving the borrower as the sole signer.

The "Death and Bankruptcy" Clause. Many private student loan contracts also have a tiny little clause, hidden away in the obscure depths of the fine print. It's written in more formal language, but it basically says that *if the cosigner or the borrower dies or declares bankruptcy, the entire balance of the loan is due immediately.* Technically, it's not a default, but if you can't pay the entire loan balance right then, the loan will go into default and collections.

Say you're the borrower, the loan is in good standing, and you're making your payments every month. You have good credit, a decent-paying job, and everything is swell. Your cosigner (a friend, a family member, or an ex-boyfriend or ex-girl-friend) declares bankruptcy and cannot get this loan discharged in the bankruptcy process, which is fairly typical given the stringent bankruptcy standards regarding student loans. You will eventually get a call from your lender, or maybe even a collections agency, telling you to pay up because the entire loan balance is due. You did nothing wrong, but you now have a defaulted student loan on your hands.

Or, even more horrifying, say your cosigner dies. While you are dealing with the emotional upheaval of losing a close friend or family member, you get a call from your lender or a collections agency: the loan is in default, and the entire loan balance is due.

These clauses do not appear in *every* private student loan contract, but they are quite common, and they should give borrowers and cosigners pause. It's certainly a reason to try to get your cosigner released, if possible, and avoid a cosigning situation in the first place.

Conclusion

Given the array of issues outlined in this chapter, it's obviously critical that you know the types of student loans that are in your portfolio if you want to fully understand your options for managing them. However, loan type is not the only thing you should be thinking about in terms of student loan management.

3

Your Student Loan Status

Your loan status determines your rights, responsibilities, and options for a particular loan at any given time. For example, while they are in school, most borrowers are able to postpone their payments through a deferment. This makes sense, since you should be focused on your education, not repaying your loans, so that you can get your degree, get that job, and repay your student loan. Sometime after graduation, though, you will be required to enter repayment. If you don't comply with your obligations based on the status of your loan, it could lead to trouble. Understanding your student loan status may seem like an obvious no-brainer, but it is a critical foundational component to loan repayment management, and while this may seem like common sense, it's worth a quick review.

Repayment

This one is fairly self-explanatory. Your loans are due, and you have to make monthly payments according to your repayment schedule.

Rights: If you can't afford your payments, you may be able to postpone them by requesting a deferment or forbearance.

Responsibilities: You have to pay your minimum monthly payment due. Partial payments will not count toward fulfilling this responsibility. Failure to pay your entire monthly payment on time can result in late fees, negative credit reporting, and possibly even default.

Options: You may have several different repayment plans to choose from, particularly for your federal student loans. Some of these plans could be based on your income, even if you have a very large loan balance. For private loans, count on only one or two repayment options (most likely based on the balance of the loan, not on your financial circumstances).

Grace Period

The *grace period* is a unique time period after graduation during which no payments are required. The idea is that lenders want to give the recent graduate time to find a job before they start sending bills.

Grace periods vary depending on your loan. Federal Stafford loans have a six-month grace period. Federal Perkins loans have a nine-month grace period. Federal Graduate PLUS loans do not technically have a grace period, but they do have a six-month post-graduation "deferment" that functions essentially as a grace period (but you may have to formally request one from your loan servicer). Federal Parent PLUS loans have **no** grace period, since the parents are responsible for payment rather than the graduate. Private student loans typically have a six-month grace period, although certain private bar study loans have a nine-month grace period.

An important thing to keep in mind regarding grace periods is **they can be used only one time**. This is especially important for graduate students and law students. If you took out student loans to fund your undergraduate degree, and you also took out student loans for law school, then you likely have used some or all of your grace periods for your undergraduate student loans, even if you went immediately into law school. This means that your undergraduate student loans may become due much sooner than your law school loans, possibly immediately after graduation (if you've used up all of the applicable grace periods).

Rights: You don't have to make payments during a grace period, but interest will still accrue on your loans.

Responsibilities: Know if you have a grace period for your loans, and know when your grace periods will end. Be proactive, and don't just wait for the first bill to arrive.

Options: You can make voluntary payments if you want to cover the interest that is accruing, but this is not required.

 TIP Navigating grace periods can be particularly challenging for law graduates, given the multitude of different student loan types that may be at issue, coupled with the burden of undergraduate loans whose grace periods may have already been depleted. Law students and recent law graduates should contact their loan servicer before or immediately after graduation to determine exactly when their loans will enter repayment—and put all of those dates on your calendar.

Deferment

Deferments allow you to postpone your payments for a certain period of time. Deferments may be granted for a variety of reasons, the most common of which is being enrolled in school at least half-time. During school, you usually don't have to make payments on your loans. Deferments can also be granted for other situations, such as unemployment or economic hardship, but this is mostly true just for federal student loans. For federal loans in deferment, interest will accrue on any unsubsidized loans (including unsubsidized Stafford loans and Graduate PLUS loans), but the interest will not be capitalized. For subsidized federal loans, such as subsidized Stafford loans and federal Perkins loans, interest may not accrue during the deferment period, which is a unique benefit.

Rights: You don't have to make payments. Federal student loan borrowers typically have 36 months of economic hardship deferment available during the repayment term of their loans.

Responsibilities: You have to meet the requirements of your particular deferment, such as remaining enrolled in school, or being unemployed.

Options: You can make voluntary payments if you want to reduce interest accrual or pay down your loan balance during the deferment period, or you can end the deferment early if your circumstances change. You can go back into deferment again later, if necessary.

Forbearance

Forbearances also allow you to postpone payments, but they are usually granted in times of hardship. Your forbearance rights vary depending on the type of loan you have, but importantly, interest continues to accrue during forbearance for all types of student loans—sometimes in a way that causes your balance to increase at a faster rate than a deferment. This is because outstanding interest may be periodically *capitalized*, meaning it is added back to your principal balance—and then interest accrues on that larger principal balance.

Rights: As with a deferment, you don't have to make payments during the forbearance period. Federal student loan borrowers typically have 36 months of economic hardship forbearance available during the repayment term of their loans.

Responsibilities: Forbearances are typically time-limited, meaning you have a finite amount of forbearance available, and you can't postpone your payments forever. Be aware of interest accrual.

Options: You can make voluntary payments if you want, and like deferment, you can end a forbearance period early if your circumstances change.

Delinquency

This is where things get a little scary. *Delinquency* means you have fallen behind on your student loan payments, but you haven't quite defaulted on your loan.

Delinquency can be dangerous: your lender or servicer may hit you with late fees, and the delinquencies may be reported to the credit bureaus, seriously damaging your credit score. You should avoid delinquency if at all possible. The good news is that when you're in delinquency status, there's usually still time to get your loan back to good standing before you go into default.

Rights: You have a right to fix the delinquency and return the loan to good standing. You may be able to do this by making the past-due payments, by obtaining a retroactive deferment or forbearance, or by consolidating your loans.

Responsibilities: You have to fix the delinquency before your loan defaults. You may have to pay late fees.

Options: You may be able to change repayment plans or postpone your payments retroactively, depending on your loan type and your overall circumstances.

Default

If you've **defaulted** on your student loan, it means that you've broken the terms of the loan contract, usually by failing to make your payments for a certain period of time. Federal student loans typically go into default after 270 days (nine months) of delinquency. Private student loans are much more variable, and the time frame for a default depends on the specific terms and conditions of the loan contract. In general, private student loans will go into default much faster than federal student loans, typically after 60 to 180 days of delinquency.

When you default on your student loan, the entire loan balance is **accelerated** and due at once. You no longer have the option to continue to repay the loan in installments. The lender may aggressively pursue you or may hire a collection agency or law firm to force you to pay. The consequences of defaulting on your loans can be quite severe. But all is not lost. There may be ways out of default (more on that later).

Rights: Even if your loans are in default, you have a right to be free from harassing, misleading, and abusive behavior from debt collectors.

Responsibilities: Technically speaking, you have to repay the entire loan balance all at once, but …

Options: You may have options to resolve the defaults for less than the full balance, or return the loans to good standing again, depending on the type of student loan that you have and your particular circumstances. We'll discuss default in more detail a bit later.

4

Student Loan Players

So far, we've covered student loan "types" and student loan "status." Both are crucial concepts. However, our initial crash course in student loans doesn't end there.

Any given student loan can seemingly involve multiple entities. If you have several student loans, as most people do, and several different *types* of loans, it can be incredibly confusing to figure out who is doing what, and what role each organization or company is playing. Understanding these different entities, and knowing what their roles are, is critical if you hope to stay on top of your student loans.

Here's a breakdown of the key players in the world of student loans.

Lender

Your *lender* is the original entity that issued you the student loan. You borrowed from the lender, you signed a promissory note provided by the lender, and you have to repay the lender. For private loans, the lender may be a private company such as a bank, a nonprofit organization, or a state agency that issues state-based student loans. The U.S. Department of Education is the lender for all Direct program federal loans, but, as mentioned before, federal loans in the FFEL program were issued by *private* lenders, including banks.

 TIP Remember, your federal student loans will appear on the NSLDS federal student loan database at www.nslds.ed.gov. Private loans will not. So if you have a student loan with a private lender and you're not sure if it is a FFEL program loan or a purely private loan, check on NSLDS. If it's listed on there, it's federal. If not, it's private. Remember, too, that the FFEL program was discontinued in 2010, so if your student loan was issued by a private lender *after* 2010, it's probably a private loan.

Sometimes, after you take out a loan, another company will purchase your student loan from the original lender. This is more common with private student loans but occurs with FFEL program loans as well. When that happens, your payments must go to the "new" lender. Although the other terms of your repayment should stay the same, administrative errors and coordination problems can sometimes cause mistakes, so it's important to keep track of who your current lender is.

It is not uncommon for loan transfers to happen multiple times over the life of a loan, particularly for private student loans.

Servicer

This is the company that manages the day-to-day operations of your loan on behalf of the lender—and for most of you, your servicer is going to be the most important entity that you deal with. Your servicer sends your monthly bills, processes payments, reviews deferment and forbearance requests, and essentially is the "face" of your student loan. You'll likely deal with your loan servicer on a regular basis, and it is critical that your servicer has up-to-date contact information for you in case there are any problems with your loan.

Your lender and your servicer are almost never the same entity, and most lenders, both federal and private, contract out the servicing operations of their student loan portfolios to a third party. For Direct federal student loans, you'll almost never deal with the U.S. Department of Education (the lender) directly; you'll most likely deal with one of its four major servicing companies: NelNet, Navient (formerly Sallie Mae), Great Lakes Higher Education, or FedLoan Servicing/PHEAA. Because lender-servicer contracts are time-limited, and student loans are repaid over long repayment terms, your loan servicer could change multiple times during the life of your loan. This makes it even more critical that your servicer has up-to-date contact information for you—that way, if a transfer does occur, you can be properly notified.

Guaranty Agency

As mentioned earlier, up until 2010, most federal loans were issued via the FFEL program: a private commercial lender originated the loans, and these loans were backed or "guaranteed" by the federal government through an entity called a guaranty agency. If a borrower defaults on a FFEL program loan, the guaranty agency repays the lender and takes over the loan. The borrower would then owe the guaranty agency. If the guaranty agency cannot adequately recover the defaulted loan, it has the authority to assign the loan, yet again, to the U.S. Department of Education.

 TIP The individual loan detail pages on the NSLDS database (at www.nslds.ed.gov) will list all of your current federal loan servicers for both Direct program loans and FFEL program loans. For FFEL program loans, the detail pages will also show the guaranty agency that will take over your loan in the event that you default.

Collection Agency

If your student loan goes into default, the lender or guaranty agency (if there is one) may initially try to get you to pay up or resolve the default. Most lenders and guaranty agencies, including the U.S. Department of Education, have internal collections departments to handle the pursuit of defaulted borrowers.

Eventually, however, most student loan lenders will outsource collections activities to a private third-party debt collection agency. Unlike other types of consumer debt, the student loan lender typically does not *sell* your loan to a debt collection agency. Instead, the lender stays in the picture, and the debt collection agency is simply the "hired gun" that goes after the defaulted borrower. Think of a collection agency as a much nastier type of loan servicer: they work for the lender or guaranty agency, but instead of simply managing the day-to-day repayment process, their job is to pressure you to repay your student loan or resolve the default. Collection agencies often push the envelope of the law, and sometimes break it altogether, while pursuing borrowers.

Some student loan companies serve multiple roles, and this can create confusion for borrowers. For example, Great Lakes Higher Education is a servicer for some Direct program federal student loans, but it's also a guaranty agency for FFEL program federal loans; it also has an internal collections department for defaulted loans and thus can act like a debt collection agency. Similarly, Navient is a private student loan lender, a private student loan servicer, and a federal student loan servicer for the Direct and FFEL programs. Untangling this web of multiple roles can be challenging. A good place to start is the NSLDS database (www.nslds.ed.gov).

5

How Interest Works

Now comes the fun part in terms of understanding the mechanics of student loans: math.

If you're terrified and bewildered by how much your student loan balance has grown over time, you're not alone. Many borrowers, particularly graduate students and law students, graduate from school with much higher loan balances than they started with. Other borrowers make payments on their student loans for many years, only to find that their balance has been only moderately reduced. How is this possible?

A big part of the answer is usually *interest*, and many people simply do not fully understand how it works.

To start, the original balance of your loan is called the *principal*. Interest is essentially a fee for borrowing money that gets added to your loan over time, and it's the main way that lenders profit from your student loan, cover administrative costs, and protect against the risks of default. There are two basic types of interest rates:

Fixed rates are interest rates that are "locked in" for the life of the loan. A fixed rate provides certainty and predictability: you know how much interest will accrue over the life of the loan, because it's just not going to change. However, there's a flip side: if you have a high fixed-rate student loan, you're stuck with it.

Variable rates change throughout the life of the loan. These rates may start off relatively low but may balloon enormously over time. This makes predicting interest accrual and the effectiveness of your loan payments exceedingly difficult. Some lenders cap the maximum allowable variable interest rate, but often those limits are quite high, meaning that borrowers may accrue enormous levels of interest during their repayment term. However, borrowers who start out with a high interest rate on a variable loan may see their rates drop, which would mean that a larger portion of their monthly payment would go toward paying down loan principal.

In addition to the *type* of interest rate you have, there's another important factor in understanding interest accrual, and that's *compounding*. Compounding occurs when interest that has accrued is *capitalized*, or added to the principal balance, and interest then continues to accrue on that larger principal balance. Then, *that* interest is subsequently capitalized, and the cycle continues. Compounding can rapidly increase your loan balance because interest accrues faster and faster over time. Compounding interest is the cornerstone of investing; Albert Einstein called it the "eighth wonder of the world." It's great when it works in your favor, but in the case of student loans, compound interest can mean massive profits for lenders and substantial losses for you.

The loan contract you signed specifies how and when interest can be capitalized and compounded. Sometimes interest is capitalized when you change your loan status, such as when you switch repayment plans or exit a forbearance period. Other times, a lender has total discretion in deciding when interest can be capitalized. Here's an example of how capitalizing and compounding interest can be costly.

Let's start with a student loan balance of $100,000 (not an atypical loan balance for a graduating law student) at a 6.8 percent interest rate (not an atypical interest rate for graduate student loans). If that interest is not capitalized, $6,800 in interest will accrue each year. Over five years, this will total $34,000 in interest, bringing the total loan balance to **$134,000**.

However, let's assume that the interest is capitalized and then compounded every year (which can happen under certain circumstances—for instance, during periods of forbearance). In the first year, $6,800 in interest will accrue, but it will be capitalized, and the loan balance will be recalculated at $106,800. Interest now accrues at the same rate, but on this larger principal balance. After the second year, $7,262 in additional interest will accrue, bringing the total loan balance to $114,062. Each year, a larger amount of interest would be added to the loan balance, meaning that more interest will accrue the following year. After five years of this cycle, the loan balance would be nearly **$139,000**. That's $5,000 higher than the prior example without capitalization and compounding.

Let's explore how this all works for a typical student loan. By way of example, let's say Sally goes to law school and takes out $100,000 in student loans. Because she is in law school, none of these loans are subsidized, so interest will accrue from day one. We'll give these loans a fixed interest rate of 6.8 percent, a fairly typical interest rate for federal student loans.

Starting Total Balance: $100,000

Step 1: While in School. Sally goes to law school for three years. For simplicity, we'll assume she took out an equal amount of student loans at the beginning of each year of law school ($33,333.33). During law school, Sally does not need to make payments, but interest is accruing: three years of interest will accrue on her first-year (1L) loans, two years of interest will accrue on her second-year (2L) loans, and one year of interest will accrue on her third-year (3L) loans. None of this interest gets capitalized while she is in school, but by the time she graduates, Sally will have accrued approximately $13,600 in interest.

New Total Balance: $113,600

Step 2: Grace Period. Sally gets a six-month grace period after she graduates to allow her to find a job and get situated. No payments are due, but interest is continuing to accrue on the original principal balance. She'll add another $3,400 in interest by the time her grace period ends.
New Total Balance: $117,000

So, before Sally has even started to repay her student loans, her total loan balance is already $117,000, or 17 percent higher than the original amounts she borrowed—all because of interest accrual.

Step 3: Forbearance. Luckily for Sally, she passes the bar exam. Unluckily for Sally, she doesn't land a full-time job until three months after her grace periods end. Because Sally can't afford to make any payments on her student loans without any income coming in, she puts her loans into a temporary three-month forbearance to postpone repayment. Another $1,700 in interest will accrue during these three months, bringing her total outstanding interest balance to $18,700. However, at the end of her forbearance period, all of this outstanding interest gets capitalized—added to the principal balance. Interest will now continue to accrue at the same rate on this larger balance.
New Total Loan Balance: $118,700

Step 4: Repayment. Finally, Sally is hired as a full-time associate at a mid-size downtown law firm. She selects a repayment plan that she can afford: an extended 25-year repayment plan with a monthly payment of $825 per month (we'll talk much more about repayment plan options later). This is pretty steep, but for a loan balance of this size, it may be one of the cheapest plans available. But keep in mind: *interest is still accruing*. With a 6.8 percent interest rate on that now-inflated balance of $118,700, more than **$670** of Sally's monthly payments will be going to interest, leaving only about **$155** to pay down the principal balance of the loan. Each month, a little less interest will accrue, and a little more of Sally's payments will go toward the principal, but it's going to take a long time for her monthly payments to break even between principal and interest. If Sally stays on the 25-year plan, she'll wind up paying a total of **$247,000** or more. That's almost two and a half times the amount she originally borrowed.

This is why interest matters, and this is why student loans can seem impossible to repay.

Unfortunately, the situation gets far worse if your interest rate is even only a little bit higher. If everything in the preceding scenario stays the same, except that this time Sally has an **8.0 percent** interest rate instead of 6.8 percent (just 1.2 percent higher), watch how drastically this will affect her loan balance and the cost of repayment:

At graduation, Sally's loan balance is **$116,000** … instead of $113,600.

After her grace period, Sally's loan balance is **$120,000** … instead of $117,000.

After her three-month forbearance, Sally's loan balance (now with the interest capitalized) is **$122,000** … instead of $118,700.

When Sally enters repayment, if she were to pay only $825 per month, **$813** will go **entirely to interest,** instead of $670. She'll barely be paying down her loan principal. To repay her loans in full within 25 years, Sally would need to make monthly payments of more than **$915**. And, in this case, at the end of 25 years, Sally will have paid a total of nearly **$275,000**, over $28,000 more than in the earlier scenario—all because of a 1.2 percent difference in the interest rate.

Summary: Original Disbursed Loan Amounts Totaling $100,000

	Interest Rate 6.8%	Interest Rate 8.0%
Starting balance	$100,000	$100,000
Balance at graduation	$113,600	$116,000
Balance after grace period	$117,000	$120,000
Balance after forbearance	$118,700	$122,000
Total amount repaid (25 years)	$247,000	$275,000

Bottom line? Interest matters.

6

Repayment Plan Programs

If you were confused about the different types of student loans, their statuses, student loan-related entities, and the mechanics of interest accrual, you're certainly not alone. Repayment plans aren't exactly straightforward and simple, either. But as all roads lead to Rome, all student loans eventually must enter repayment.

Federal Loan Repayment

Typically—and unfortunately—private student loan borrowers will have very limited repayment plan options. Most private lenders offer one repayment plan; if you're lucky, your lender may offer you a second option. Private loan borrowers essentially give you a choice: repay your loans under the plan that you're provided, or risk delinquency and default.

When it comes to paying back your federal student loans, however, borrowers have many choices. So many choices, in fact, with so many overlapping considerations and confusing eligibility criteria, that it can be a bit overwhelming to decide on a particular plan. Some plans have lower monthly payments, but the tradeoff is a longer repayment term and a greater amount paid in total over the life of the loan. Other repayment plans may be tied to your income, regardless of the loan balance.

 TIP If you are currently in repayment and don't know what repayment plan you are on, you can contact your loan servicer; they should be able to tell you.

Let's stick with Sally at the time that she enters repayment. Remember, after her graduation, grace period, and forbearance, her loans (at a 6.8 percent interest rate) enter repayment with a total balance of $118,700. We'll look at the various repayment plans to understand her options:

Balance-based level repayment plans are based on the loan balance and interest rate, with monthly payments spread out evenly over time. The repayment term can vary from 10 to 30 years, depending on the loan program. Plans with longer repayment terms have lower monthly payments but cost more in total because it takes longer to pay the loan off, and the borrower therefore pays more in interest.

For Sally, the 10-year plan would cost her roughly **$1,370** per month. Over 10 years, she would pay approximately **$164,000**. A plan with a 25-year repayment term instead of 10 would cost Sally just **$825** per month (a bargain!), but by the end of the repayment term, she will have paid approximately **$247,000**.

Balance-based graduated repayment plans, like the level plans, are also based on the loan balance and interest rate, but monthly payments change over the course of the repayment term. At the beginning of the repayment term, monthly payments are fairly low. Then the payments gradually ramp up over time to compensate for the lower initial payments. Many borrowers on these plans will pay more over the life of the loan than they would under the level repayment plan options. Graduated repayment plan terms can be 10, 25, or 30 years.

On a 10-year graduated repayment plan, Sally's monthly payment would start at approximately **$790** but would gradually increase to nearly **$2,365** toward the end of the repayment term. After 10 years, she would have paid approximately **$176,000**. For the 25-year version, her payment would start at approximately **$675** but would increase to nearly **$1,180** during the last few years of the repayment term. By the end, she will have paid nearly **$268,000**, making this plan one of the most expensive in terms of the total dollar amount paid.

Graduated repayment options are designed to ease the burden on new graduates, but the price for early relief is higher payments down the line and a larger amount paid in total.

Income-driven repayment plans are entirely different from the balance-based plans. Instead of focusing on the loan balance and interest rate to achieve a full payoff of the loan, income-driven plans use a formula to calculate a unique monthly payment based on the borrower's financial circumstances. The plans look at a borrower's *discretionary income*, which is generally defined as the amount of a borrower's *adjusted gross income* (as reported on his or her tax return) above 150 percent of the poverty limit for the borrower's family size.[1] If any balance remains at the conclusion of the plan's repayment term, it is forgiven, although the forgiven amount may be treated as taxable income (which could cause some borrowers to be left with a huge tax liability ... more on that later).

For many borrowers with large federal student loan balances, income-driven plans are the only affordable repayment plans. Nevertheless, each of these plans utilizes a somewhat different formula, and they have unique eligibility requirements, making it a bit challenging for borrowers to select the ideal plan.

The Income-Contingent Repayment (ICR) plan was the original long-term income-driven repayment plan for borrowers with high debt burdens relative to their incomes. This plan is available only for Direct federal student loans, meaning that FFEL program loans and Perkins loans are not eligible.

---

1 Note: "Discretionary income" for the Income-Contingent Repayment (ICR) plan, in contrast to the other income-driven plans, is defined as a borrower's adjusted gross income above *100 percent* (as opposed to 150 percent) of the poverty limit for the borrower's family size.

Under ICR, monthly payments for eligible loans are capped at 20 percent of the borrower's discretionary income. The repayment period is up to 25 years. If the loans are not repaid in full within those 25 years, any balance that remains is forgiven. If Sally is single, has an adjusted gross income of $65,000, and enrolls in ICR, her monthly payment will be approximately **$890**. The payments will be adjusted each year as Sally's income changes. If her adjusted gross income increases to $80,000, her monthly payment will be approximately **$1,140**.

TIP For most student loan borrowers, ICR is not going to be the ideal option for income-driven repayment because ICR's formula would result in a higher monthly payment compared to the newer income-driven repayment plans discussed later. It's important to be aware that ICR exists, but the only borrowers who should be selecting ICR are Parent PLUS loan borrowers who consolidate with a Direct Consolidation loan; Parent PLUS borrowers are otherwise "locked out" of the remaining income-driven repayment plans.

Right now, the *Income-Based Repayment (IBR) plan* is the most widely available and used income-driven repayment plan option. IBR is designed for borrowers with high federal student debt balances compared to their incomes, and the program was created as a more favorable alternative to ICR, which saddled low-income borrowers with payments that were still quite high. IBR works similarly to ICR but uses a different formula to calculate the monthly payment: instead of your payment being based on 20 percent of your discretionary income, it's 15 percent. Furthermore, Direct program loans and FFEL program loans are all eligible for IBR, making it much more accessible (note that Perkins loans cannot be repaid under IBR, however).

Like ICR, the repayment period for IBR is up to 25 years. If the loans are not paid off within those 25 years, any balance that remains is forgiven—although, as with all of the income-driven repayment plans, the amount forgiven may be treated as taxable income.

There is a newer version of IBR that has a lower monthly payment (10 percent of discretionary income instead of 15 percent) and a shorter repayment term (20 years instead of 25 years). However, this version of IBR is available only to "new borrowers" as of July 1, 2014. In other words, you must not have had any outstanding federal student loan balance as of July 1, 2014, and you must have taken out new federal student loans on or after this date, as well. Practically speaking, this means that as of the writing of this book, very few (if any) borrowers are currently eligible for this version of IBR. Assuming that a law student takes out federal loans during each year of a typical three-year legal education, the soonest law graduates will be able to access this "IBR for new borrowers" will be in 2017 (assuming no outstanding undergraduate federal student loans).

For Sally, entering repayment with an adjusted gross income of $65,000 and a household size of one, she would make monthly payments of approximately **$595** if she enrolled in IBR. This is, obviously, significantly cheaper than ICR as well as any of the balance-based repayment plan options, and may be the only affordable repayment plan available to her. If her income increases to $80,000, her monthly IBR payment will increase to approximately **$780**; higher, to be sure, but still manageable.

TIP Under IBR, your loan servicer will consider your joint income if you are married and file joint tax returns with your spouse. However, your loan servicer will consider your individual income if you file taxes separately from your spouse. Thus, for some married couples, there may be an incentive to file taxes separately, as it can reduce monthly household IBR payments. However, there may be drawbacks to filing separate tax returns in the form of higher taxes. You and your spouse will want to consult with a qualified tax expert to weigh any potential student loan repayment savings achievable by filing taxes separately against the tax consequences.

Pay-As-You-Earn (PAYE) is a new repayment plan that was recently created by the Obama administration. It is very similar to IBR but has two important differences: (1) it has lower monthly payments than IBR because the formula calculates your monthly payment as 10 percent of your discretionary income, as compared to 15 percent under IBR and 20 percent under ICR; and (2) it has a shorter repayment term of 20 years, instead of 25 years. Thus, PAYE is a significantly better alternative to IBR.

However, the plan has strict eligibility requirements:

- Only Direct federal loans are eligible. FFEL loans, Perkins loans, and Parent PLUS loans are ineligible for PAYE.
- You must have had no outstanding federal student loan as of October 1, 2007. In other words, as of this date you must have either never taken out federal student loans, or you must have repaid them already.
- You must have received a new Direct federal student loan disbursement on or after October 1, 2011. Obtaining a Direct consolidation does not count as a new "disbursement."

The loan disbursement date restrictions just described are the U.S. Department of Education's way of limiting the PAYE plan to what it considers "new borrowers." If you're just graduating law school now and never took out student loans prior to law school, you may very well be eligible for the PAYE plan. Borrowers who have been in repayment for a while, or took out loans prior to law school, may not be eligible for this plan.

If Sally can get onto PAYE, this plan will provide her with the lowest possible monthly payments. With an adjusted gross income of $65,000, Sally's monthly payment would be around **$395**. Even when her income increases to $80,000 per year, her payments would remain reasonable: **$520/month**. This is still cheaper than any of the balance-based repayment plan options, given her loan balance and interest rate.

TIP Much like IBR, for the PAYE plan your loan servicer will consider your joint income if you are married and file joint tax returns with your spouse. However, your loan servicer will consider only your individual income if you file taxes separately from your spouse.

Revised Pay-As-You-Earn (REPAYE). The graduated repayment plans were implemented to give borrowers an alternative to the level repayment plans, as most borrowers will enter repayment on the lowest end of their earning potential. ICR was designed to be an improvement over the increasingly expensive balance-based repayment programs (both level and graduated). As average student loan debt increased, IBR was created as an alternative to ICR. And when even IBR wasn't providing enough relief to borrowers, PAYE was created.

But, as described previously, PAYE is the most limited of the repayment plan options, given its strict eligibility requirements. So, in the summer of 2014, the Obama administration announced that it would be creating a new version of the PAYE plan to make it more accessible to borrowers who are barred from the program because of the disbursement dates of their loans.

Enter the Revised Pay-As-You-Earn (REPAYE) plan, which was announced and named following several rounds of negotiated rulemaking sessions that concluded in the spring of 2015. The plan was formally implemented in December of 2015. REPAYE is the same plan as PAYE in terms of the formula used to calculate monthly payments (10 percent of discretionary income). REPAYE is available only to Direct loan borrowers, but it eliminates the "new borrower" loan disbursement date restrictions that make PAYE inaccessible to most federal student loan borrowers currently in repayment. However, there are many new elements to REPAYE that make it significantly different from PAYE, IBR, and even ICR:

- REPAYE has *two* possible repayment terms. Under REPAYE, for borrowers who took out student loans only for their undergraduate education, the repayment term is 20 years. Any remaining balance is forgiven at that time. For borrowers who took out student loans for their graduate education (such as law school), the repayment term is 25 years, and any remaining balance is then forgiven. This differs from the other income-driven plans, in which the repayment terms are 20 years (for PAYE) and 25 years (for IBR and ICR), regardless of the educational program.
- Under the ICR, IBR, and PAYE plans, a borrower who is married and files taxes separately from his or her spouse can base the monthly payment on the borrower's income alone. This is a big deal for married couples where one spouse

has significantly higher federal student loan debt than the other spouse, but much lower income. Under REPAYE, however, federal loan servicers will consider your *joint marital income, regardless of whether you file taxes jointly or separately from your spouse.* This may make REPAYE a non-starter for some married borrowers, even with the more favorable payment calculation formula.

Income-Driven Repayment Plan Summary

	Monthly Payment	Eligible Loans	Repayment Period	Forgiven Balance Is Taxable Income	Married Filing Taxes Separately
Income-Contingent Repayment (ICR)	20% of discretionary income	Federal Direct	25 years	Yes	Borrower's income only
Income-Based Repayment (IBR)	15% of discretionary income	Federal Direct and FFEL	25 years	Yes	Borrower's income only
Income-Based Repayment (IBR) for "New Borrowers"	10% of discretionary income	Federal Direct and FFEL	20 years	Yes	Borrower's income only
Pay-As-You-Earn (PAYE)	10% of discretionary income	Federal Direct (additional eligibility criteria also apply)	20 years	Yes	Borrower's income only
Revised Pay-As-You-Earn (REPAYE)	10% of discretionary income	Federal Direct	20 years (undergradu-ate), 25 years (graduate)	Yes	Borrower and spouse combined income

Repayment Plan Summary Chart
(Assuming a starting loan balance of $118,700 at a 6.8% interest rate)

Repayment Plan	Initial Monthly Payment
Standard—10 years	$1,370
Extended—25 years	$825
Graduated—10 years	$790
Graduated—25 years	$675
ICR, AGI $65,000 and family size of 1	$890
ICR, AGI $80,000 and family size of 1	$1,140
IBR, AGI $65,000 and family size of 1	$595
IBR, AGI $80,000 and family size of 1	$780
PAYE and REPAYE, AGI $65,000 and family size of 1	$395
PAYE and REPAYE, AGI $80,000 and family size of 1	$520

But What About Interest?

Under any repayment plan, interest continues to accrue during the repayment period. Every monthly payment that you make is being divided between principal and ongoing interest accrual.

Under the income-driven repayment plan options, interest accrual can be a bit more terrifying. Your monthly ICR, IBR, PAYE, or REPAYE payment may be *lower* than the interest that accrues each month. Sally's $118,700 loan will still accrue interest at a rate of 6.8 percent, which works out to roughly **$670 per month**, *regardless of the payment plan she is on.* That means that with an adjusted gross income of $65,000, her monthly payments under *all* of the income-driven plans (except for ICR) would not cover all of her interest accrual. Thus, her loan balance may actually *increase* over time, even though she's responsibly making payments according to the terms of the repayment program she selected. This process, in which your overall balance continues to grow even when you make your required income-driven payments, is called **negative amortization**.

The underlying goal of income-driven repayment is to make payments that are affordable, regardless of your loan balance, until your loans are paid off or forgiven at 20 or 25 years. However, it can be frightening to see your loan balance increase, and with the prospect of having your forgiven loans treated as taxable income at the conclusion of the repayment term, you should monitor your payments and your loan balance over time and, if necessary, prepare for a looming tax bill.

Recertifying Your Income Annually

For all of the income-driven repayment plans, your calculated monthly payment lasts for only 12 months at a time. You have to renew your plan annually by supplying new income information so that your monthly payment amount can be recalculated. Your loan servicer is supposed to notify you 90 days prior to the expiration of your 12-month period and give you instructions on how to reapply and submit new income documentation. Most of the time, this can be done online through a fairly easy application process.

 TIP The federal government has an online portal to recertify your income for the income-driven repayment plans. Check out www.studentloans.gov.

Sometimes, federal student loan servicers fail to send the 90-day notices to borrowers informing them that it's time to renew their income-driven repayment plans. It's best to know the month that your income-driven payment period expires and to contact your loan servicer if you have not heard from them 60 to 90 days prior to the deadline.

Conclusion

Understanding these federal student loan repayment plans is going to be absolutely critical in determining the best strategy for managing your student loans. Bookmark this chapter—you may want to circle back here as you explore Part 2 of this book.

7

Student Loan Management Programs

Determining your optimal repayment plan can be a daunting task. But repayment plans aren't the only thing to be thinking about when it comes to managing your student loans. There are numerous programs and options available to borrowers that can make student loan repayment easier, regardless of the specific repayment plan that you select. While all of these programs may not be necessary or even ideal, depending on your specific circumstances, they are all worthy of review and careful consideration. We've discussed some of them already.

Deferment and Forbearance

Deferments and forbearance programs allow borrowers to postpone their payments for various reasons, usually due to some sort of hardship. For example, if you have an unexpected expense during a particular month, you lose your job, or you sustain an injury or illness that temporarily puts you out of commission, you may not be able to afford your student loan payments for a brief period. Under such circumstances, a deferment or forbearance can give you a "free pass" on your student loan repayment obligations so you don't have to pay but you avoid delinquency and default.

Although these programs can provide crucial short-term relief for student loan borrowers, they are poor long-term strategies for managing your loans. Deferment and forbearance options are generously available for federal student loans but are usually much more restrictive for private loans.

For federal student loans, the main difference between deferment and forbearance is the handling of interest. During certain federal deferment periods, interest does not accrue for subsidized federal loans, and interest charged on unsubsidized loans doesn't get capitalized. In contrast, during a forbearance period, interest continues to accrue on all of your loans (subsidized and unsubsidized), and it will likely be capitalized; this means that your loan balance will increase more and more quickly the longer you remain in forbearance. Private student loan forbearances work in much the same way, but you may also incur an additional forbearance fee.

Be careful with forbearance. Extended periods of forbearance can cause your loan balance to increase dramatically because of interest accrual.

Few borrowers are thoroughly counseled on the interest consequences of going into long-term forbearance. Too often, borrowers use forbearance to push off paying their loans for as long as possible. It can be easy to forget about your loans when you don't have to make any payments on them, but while you're not paying much attention, interest is accruing, and your balance is increasing.

Let's look at an example. We'll take a $50,000 student loan with a 6.8 percent interest rate and put it into forbearance:

- After 6 months, the balance grows to approximately $51,700.
- After 12 months, the balance grows to approximately $53,400.
- After 24 months, the balance grows to approximately $56,800.
- After 36 months, the balance grows to approximately $60,200.

Most federal loan forbearances are time-limited and cannot be extended after 36 months. So, in the preceding example, the borrower bought three years of post-poned payments at a price of more than $10,000, which is 20 percent of his original loan balance. Furthermore, the interest that accumulated during the forbearance period will now be capitalized (added to the principal), and interest will continue to accrue at 6.8 percent on that higher total balance. This will cause the overall balance to continue to grow faster, and it requires larger monthly payments to pay it down.

For most people, forbearance makes sense only as a short-term measure, and it's okay to use it during a true emergency. But as soon as it's possible, get onto a repayment plan that results in the payoff of your loan, or an income-driven repay-ment plan with an affordable payment schedule and eventual loan forgiveness. Otherwise you're simply postponing the inevitable while adding more and more interest to the overall loan balance—and you might be shocked at how much it will cost you.

Consolidation

Consolidation allows you to combine a bunch of individual student loans into a single new loan. Put another way, consolidation results in a new, large loan that pays off several smaller ones. The main benefit of consolidation is that it can simplify loan repayment by giving you a single student loan, a single loan servicer, and a single monthly payment.

For federal student loans, there is a federal ***Direct consolidation loan program*** that allows you to consolidate your federal student loans, but *only* your federal student loans. The resulting Direct federal consolidation loan is essentially the sum of its parts, with no real change to the overall interest rate or the key terms and conditions. Specifically, a Direct loan consolidation won't lower your overall interest rate—the interest rate will be the weighted average of the loans it pays off. However, Direct loan consolidation can simplify repayment if you have multiple federal student loans with multiple federal loan servicing companies. Direct loan consolidation can also potentially open up a few new federal repayment plan options, such as the ICR, PAYE, and REPAYE income-driven repayment plan programs, as well as special 30-year standard and graduated balance-based level repayment plans, by converting all of your loans to a "Direct" program loan; this is particularly important for borrowers who have a mix of Direct and FFEL program loans, and have loan balances that exceed $60,000 (which is required to be eligible for the 30-year balance-based plans).

There are also other considerations regarding federal Direct loan consolidation that are important, however. You *cannot* include your private student loans in a Direct federal consolidation loan, which is one of the big limitations of this program. Furthermore, if you have already spent a significant amount of time in repayment on your existing federal loans, you should know that consolidation restarts the clock on your repayment term, since consolidation technically results in a new loan. This could mean that you'll pay more in total over time. For example, if your individual federal student loans had been on a 25-year extended repayment plan, and you then consolidated your loans five years into that plan and placed your new Direct consolidation loan onto a 25-year extended plan, you would be in repayment for 30 years in total (the five prior years, plus a new 25-year term). Another potential drawback of consolidation is that all loans lose any individual benefits they might have once you consolidate them. Most federal loans do not have special benefits that make it worth it to keep them separated. However, federal Perkins loans do have special cancellation options for certain professions (discussed in Chapter 8), so you'll want to take a look at your career track before deciding whether to include your Perkins loans in a federal consolidation loan.

TIP If you have Parent PLUS loans, be careful about including them in your consolidation loan if you want to select the Income-Based Repayment (IBR) plan, the Pay-As-You-Earn (PAYE) plan, or the Revised Pay-As-You-Earn (REPAYE) plan. Parent PLUS loans are not eligible for those repayment plans even if you consolidate them. If you consolidate Parent PLUS loans with other federal student loans, it could potentially make the entire consolidation loan ineligible for IBR, PAYE, and REPAYE.

Consolidating your federal loans through the Direct consolidation loan program is a fairly straightforward process, at least in theory (whenever you are dealing with large bureaucracies, there's always a chance things can go a little wrong).

You can submit a federal Direct consolidation loan application online or on paper. Applications usually take about 30 to 60 days to process but can sometimes take a little longer. Once approved, there is no grace period for the new consolidation loan; it enters repayment as soon it is issued, and payments are usually due the following month. You will have to select a repayment plan for your loan from the available options, and you are required to submit your repayment plan application along with your consolidation application.

 TIP   To learn more about federal Direct loan consolidation, visit www.studentloans.gov.

There are some private student loan consolidation programs, too. Many of these programs allow you to consolidate your private student loans *and* your federal student loans. These consolidation programs can significantly simplify repayment management if you have multiple student loans with multiple loan holders, and some of these programs may offer reduced interest rates, especially if the bulk of your loans are federal graduate student loans (like Graduate PLUS loans) and high-interest private loans. However, I generally caution people about including federal student loans in a private consolidation loan. Once a federal loan is rolled into a private consolidation loan, it ceases to be federal, and you will consequently lose out on all federal student loan program benefits such as income-driven repayment, loan forgiveness, and generous federal deferment and forbearance programs. And since there's no way to "un-consolidate" a student loan or include a private student loan in a federal Direct consolidation, it's a one-way street out of the federal student loan system.

Refinancing

Refinancing a student loan specifically means lowering the loan's interest rate, usually by taking out a new student loan with a lower interest rate to pay off and replace the loan with the higher rate. Refinancing can also act as a consolidation if you are including multiple student loans in the refinancing program and you wind up with a single new loan.

For federal student loans, there is no true refinancing mechanism within the federal student loan system. As noted earlier, the federal Direct consolidation program is an interest-neutral option, as the interest rate of a Direct consolidation loan is the weighted average of the loans included in the consolidation; thus, it can't really be called a refinancing program. It can, however, open up some new repayment plan options for certain borrowers. Senator Elizabeth Warren proposed a bill to allow federal student loan borrowers to refinance their loans within the federal student loan system to lower their interest rate, and other politicians have followed suit or supported similar bills. However, none of these proposals have passed, and it doesn't look like any of them will become viable anytime soon.

As for private student loan refinancing, options mostly dried up following the 2007–2009 financial crisis, but since 2012 there has been a slow but steady increase in refinancing options available to borrowers. As with consolidation, many of these programs allow borrowers to refinance private student loans, federal student loans, or both. But, as with private student loan consolidation, I would caution people about refinancing federal student loans via a private student loan. A lower interest rate is attractive and important, but borrowers should consider whether losing out on federal student loan program benefits is worth it. This really comes down to the borrower's goals, circumstances, and tolerance for risk.

Auto-Debit

Auto-debit can be a great way to stay on top of your student loan payments, especially when you are dealing with multiple lenders or servicers. You link your student loan accounts with your checking account, and the payments are deducted automatically. It can be a good idea: your payments are made for you, and you don't even have to think about it or worry about being late. But be careful. Auto-debit can lead to problems if you're not paying attention.

First, the good stuff. Ultimately, the goal of auto-debit is to make sure that payments are made on time. This benefits the lender, who wants your money, and the borrower, who doesn't want to get hit by late fees and a damaged credit report. For the most part, auto-debit works well as a student loan management tool, particularly for those who find it challenging to keep track of multiple monthly bill obligations. Furthermore, many federal and private loan servicers offer modest but measurable interest-reduction incentives for borrowers who sign up for auto-debit programs.

Still, auto-debit is not perfect. Sometimes a payment doesn't go through because of an issue with your bank or the loan servicing company. Sometimes the wrong amount is debited. This is especially true when borrowers are on some sort of time-limited repayment plan, such as an income-driven or reduced-payment plan that requires periodic recertification. If you don't recertify your income or submit the required paperwork, your monthly payment could skyrocket; if you're not aware of it because you haven't been paying attention, that automatic payment could clean out or overdraw your bank account, which could lead to low-balance or overdraft fees from the bank. Likewise, if a payment doesn't go through and you miss your due date, you may get hit with late fees and a negative mark on your credit report, even if it wasn't entirely your fault. You may even default on the loan if the problem goes unnoticed for an extended period of time, which is serious business.

Auto-debit is helpful, but it's not an excuse to be asleep at the wheel. Failure to regularly monitor your account can lead to serious consequences if there are unnoticed changes or problems, and it can be very difficult to correct these issues after the incidents have occurred. So, if you're going to use auto-debit, just make it a habit to regularly check your student loan account and bank account to be sure everything is functioning properly, and contact your loan servicer immediately if you notice any problems.

Conclusion

The programs described in this chapter can make your life easier by simplifying and streamlining your student loan repayment. Consider them, and contact your loan servicer for more information.

8

Loan Forgiveness Programs

Is it possible to get your student loans forgiven? Yes. But not everyone is eligible, and not all loans are eligible, either. Most private student loans have no forgiveness options at all, at least not directly, and loan forgiveness programs for federal loans have tricky eligibility requirements.

Nevertheless, loan forgiveness programs really do exist, and they can be hugely beneficial to student borrowers, especially those with heavy student loan debt burdens like law graduates. Here's an overview of some of the most important programs for attorneys.

Repayment Plan-Based Loan Forgiveness

As described earlier, federal income-driven repayment plans have their own built-in loan forgiveness provisions. Income-Based Repayment (IBR) and Income-Contingent Repayment (ICR) both provide for loan forgiveness of any remaining balance after 25 years of repayment in the program.[1] The newer Pay-As-You Earn (PAYE) repayment program provides for loan forgiveness of any remaining balance after 20 years of repayment in the program. The Revised Pay-As-You-Earn (REPAYE) program provides for loan forgiveness after 20 years of repayment if your loans were disbursed only for your undergraduate education, and after 25 years if you took out *any* federal student loans for your graduate education.

Remember that under current law, the loans forgiven under these programs may be treated as taxable income, which would be a potentially significant consequence for some borrowers. There is growing recognition in policymaking circles of the absurdity of saddling student loan borrowers with massive tax liabilities after being in affordable income-driven repayment plans for two decades or more, and there is plenty of time for lawmakers to clarify the tax consequences of loan forgiveness before the bulk of borrowers start getting their loans forgiven under these programs. Nevertheless, it is important to be aware of the potential tax issues tied to repayment-plan-based loan forgiveness.

---

1 As referenced earlier, the "IBR for new borrowers" plan, not yet available for most borrowers, allows for loan forgiveness after 20 years of repayment.

Public Service Loan Forgiveness (PSLF)

The *Public Service Loan Forgiveness (PSLF)* program is probably the best-known and most-discussed loan forgiveness program currently available. It provides for the complete forgiveness of a borrower's federal loan balance after 10 years of repayment if the borrower works full time in qualifying public service employment. Here are the key components of the program:

- **The right type of loan.** Only Direct federal loans are eligible. Non-Direct federal loans, such as FFEL and Perkins loans, are not eligible. If you have a mix of Direct program loans and non-Direct federal loans, and you intend on getting on track for the PSLF program, you can consolidate your federal loans via the federal Direct consolidation loan program and thus convert all of your loans into a Direct loan, making them eligible for PSLF.
- **The right type of repayment.** You must make 120 individual on-time payments under the ICR, IBR, PAYE, or REPAYE repayment plans. Payments made under the balance-based plans generally do not count, except for the 10-year level repayment plan, which results in the full payoff of your loans after 10 years anyway.
- **The right type of employment.** You must have full-time employment, defined as at least 30 hours per week, for either a government entity (such as a government agency or a public school) or a registered 501(c)(3) nonprofit organization, or certain other nonprofits (excluding labor unions, partisan political organizations, and organizations engaged primarily in religious-based work). You can also cobble together several part-time public service positions if you work at least 30 hours per week in total doing qualifying public service work.

PSLF is not a repayment program, as it has no impact on your monthly payment. PSLF should also not be thought of as a "10-year" program; rather, it is a "120-payment" program. In other words, you have to meet *all* of the previously listed eligibility requirements for *each individual monthly payment*, 120 times, to get your loans forgiven under the program. If you do wind up meeting all of the eligibility criteria, PSLF simply allows loan forgiveness to kick in much earlier than for the "normal" IBR, ICR, PAYE, and REPAYE loan forgiveness terms. Note that because PSLF is a "120-payment" program, you do not need to work in public service for 10 *consecutive* years; you can leave public service, and then come back to it at a later point. You would continue on your income-based repayment plan during the break, but those payments would not count toward your 120 payments needed for forgiveness.

There are two major benefits of the PSLF program. First, there is the obvious benefit that eligible borrowers can get their loans forgiven much more quickly than the repayment-based forgiveness programs described earlier. Second, under current law, that forgiven balance will not be treated as taxable income. This can be a huge incentive for borrowers with large federal student loan balances to work in public service. Although the eligibility requirements can be a little tricky, and you must meet all of these requirements for 120 payments over the course of 10 years or more, a lot of borrowers stand to benefit from this, as long as they do everything right.

 TIP For more information on Public Service Loan Forgiveness, you can check out FedLoan Servicing at www.MyFedLoan.org, which has some good information on program eligibility, as well as forms you and your employer can complete and submit to track your progress.

Perkins Loan Cancellation

Federal Perkins loans are special and have their own provisions allowing for full or partial cancellation if you work in certain specialized professions in education, health care, law enforcement, the military, the Peace Corps or AmeriCorps, or certain positions in government. For attorneys, public defenders and prosecuting attorneys stand to benefit the most from Perkins loan cancellation options. These attorneys can get a portion of their Perkins loans canceled each year that they remain in qualifying employment, and they can ultimately get their full Perkins loan balances forgiven, without having to make any payments at all, after five years of service.

 TIP Remember that if you consolidate your federal student loans via the Direct consolidation loan program, the included loans lose any unique benefits that they may have. Thus, if you anticipate working as a public defender or prosecutor, or any of the other Perkins cancellation-eligible professions, it may be prudent to exclude your Perkins loan from a consolidation loan.

Employer-Based Loan Forgiveness

While the previously discussed loan forgiveness programs are tied to professional fields and are available only via federal student loan programs, specific employers may offer loan forgiveness as well. For example, the National Institutes of Health and the National Health Service Corps both offer generous loan forgiveness and repayment assistance to employees who meet certain criteria. Peace Corps and AmeriCorps volunteers may be eligible for forgiveness or cancellation of interest for their federal student loans while serving, and AmeriCorps members may receive a lump-sum financial award that they can apply toward federal and private student loan payments. Certain private employers, including some law firms, may also offer some limited loan forgiveness and repayment assistance programs, and these programs may not even be limited to federal student loans. Check with your employer to see if any loan forgiveness or repayment assistance programs are available to you.

School-Based Loan Repayment Assistance

Many schools, particularly law schools, offer their graduates loan repayment assistance, which is essentially loan forgiveness in a different form. These programs are typically called *loan repayment assistance programs (LRAPs)*. Most LRAPs are profession-dependent, meaning that borrowers are eligible only if they work in certain public service fields, *pro bono* positions, or jobs in underserved communities.

LRAPs usually work by providing annual or semiannual lump-sum payments to borrowers that can be used toward their student loan obligations. Depending on the specific program, LRAPs may act essentially as a gift. For other programs, the LRAP payments may start off as a "loan" that you can use to pay your student loan bills (federal or private); then, as long as you remain eligible for the program, the "loan" converts to a grant that you never have to repay. Check with your school's financial aid office to see if the school offers any loan repayment assistance or forgiveness programs, and what the eligibility requirements are.

 You can find a list of law schools that offer LRAP-like programs at www. equaljusticeworks.org.

9

Default Prevention and Resolution

So far we've focused on how to manage your student loans effectively so you can keep them in good standing. Hopefully we've put you on a manageable track to paying off your loans, even in difficult financial situations. But what happens if you start falling behind on your payments?

First, you enter a loan status called *delinquency*. You may be subjected to late fees, and the delinquency may be reported to the credit bureaus, which can hurt your credit score. But the good news is that delinquency is generally fixable. You can catch up on your payments, obtain a deferment or forbearance if you are eligible, or potentially switch repayment plans.

If you can't fix the delinquency, you will eventually *default* on your loans. Defaulting means that you've broken the loan contract. Typically, the entire balance of your loan becomes due immediately in one lump sum (this is called *acceleration*). For private student loans, default can sometimes occur after only a few months of delinquency, depending on your loan contract. For most federal student loans, delinquency typically lasts for 270 days (nine months) before you formally enter default status. Delinquency means you are behind on your payment obligations by any amount—so even if you were to make a payment or two during the delinquency period, unless you *fully* get caught up on your past-due payments, you would remain in delinquency status, and you will eventually default.

The consequences of default are serious. Not only is the entire balance due at once, but additional fees and penalties may be added to your loan balance. The defaults are reported to credit bureaus, which will negatively affect your credit score, and you may be subject to collections actions and even a lawsuit. The specific consequences of a student loan default depend on the type of student loan that you are dealing with.

Federal Loan Default

Federal student loans are a very special type of debt. We're taught that a college and graduate education is necessary to get ahead in life, and, unless you come from serious wealth or get a merit scholarship, the ticket to that ride is paid for with student loans. Nearly all financial aid award packages from law schools include at least some federal student loans.

At the time, it's easy: all you have to do is sign. But while all loans have a dark side for borrowers who default, federal lenders have enormous powers to aggressively pursue you:

- Without a court order, the federal government or federal loan guarantor can garnish your wages.
- Without a court order, the federal government can seize your tax refund if one is due to you and apply it to your federal loan balance.
- Without a court order, the federal government can seize a certain portion of federal benefits, such as Social Security or other federal money owed to you.
- Federal law authorizes government-contracted private debt collection agencies to tack on exorbitant "collections costs" of up to 25 percent of the total defaulted loan balance. This is how collections agencies profit off of defaulted borrowers. Even if you can resolve your defaults, you may be legally responsible for the additional costs that are added to your loans.
- You are prohibited from obtaining new federal financial aid while you are in default. So if you defaulted on your federal student loans while you were in school, you may be in big trouble if you rely on financial aid to complete your degree.
- There is no statute of limitations on the collection of federal student loans, which means the government can pursue you for the rest of your life. So, if your wages are being garnished and you cannot resolve the default, the garnishment may continue until the loan is completely paid off.
- The federal government or federal loan guaranty agency can sue you in court. With a judgment from a court of law, the federal lender has even more powers to pursue you, such as putting a lien on any property you own or seizing money from your bank account.

These consequences are, of course, in addition to the negative impact on your credit report. Delinquencies and defaults are both reported to the credit bureaus, and your credit score will take a significant hit as a result. A lower credit score and an active defaulted debt can be a significant barrier to employment, housing, and new credit. It can even jeopardize professional licensure in certain cases—including a license to practice law.

The good news is that despite these draconian collection powers and consequences, there are limits on what the federal government and collection agencies can do. If debt collectors are threatening you with something that sounds completely outside the scope of what we've just discussed, you may want to consider hiring an attorney who specializes in consumer protection and debt collection to help.

Private Loan Default

There are fundamental differences between federal and private student loans in default. Private lenders are much more limited than the federal government in what they can do to collect from you without a court order. They cannot simply choose to garnish your wages or seize federal money that is owed to you. Your private student loans will still likely be placed with a private debt collection agency, and your credit will still be significantly damaged, but the private lender has limited options to *force* you to pay until it gets a court order.

However, this means that private lenders have a greater incentive to sue defaulted borrowers than the federal government. With a judgment from a court, a private lender can use the power of the court to pursue you. The exact powers and effects of a judgment vary from state to state, but a private student loan lender may be able to enforce the judgment by garnishing your wages, seizing bank accounts, or putting a lien on your property. Furthermore, as with federal student loan default, your delinquencies and defaults will be reported to the major credit bureaus.

 If you are in default or collections, now may be a good time to consider hiring an attorney to assist you—even if you are an attorney yourself. Consumer law in general and student loan law in particular are fairly specialized niche practices. A good place to start would be the National Association of Consumer Advocates, which has a directory on its website: www.consumeradvocates.org.

Avoiding Default

Default can obviously be terrifying and destructive to your life, and it is best avoided if at all possible. If you're falling behind on monthly payments, you may have some options to pull your loans back from the brink.

Deferment or Forbearance

If you are unable to make any payments because of an economic hardship, then postponing your payments through deferment or forbearance would be preferable to defaulting. Contact your loan servicer for details on what options you have. If you just lost your job, you may be eligible for an unemployment deferment for your federal student loans. If you are just having a tough time financially, economic hardship forbearance might be available for both your federal and private student loans. Just be careful: deferment and forbearance periods do not last forever, and you will eventually have to get back onto a regular repayment plan. Only use deferment and forbearance in emergencies, and return to a payment plan as soon as you can.

Income-Driven Repayment

If your loans are federal and you find yourself falling behind, take a look at your repayment plan. You may be eligible for one of the income-driven repayment plan options (ICR, IBR, PAYE, or REPAYE), which could result in a more manageable repayment situation. If you're not too far behind, your loan servicer may even be able to give you a courtesy non-interest-capitalization forbearance called an *administrative forbearance* to cancel out your past-due balance while your income-driven repayment request is processed.

Consolidation

For federal student loans, you may find that consolidation is a good option. As described earlier, consolidation can simplify loan repayment management by combining all of your federal loans into one. Consolidation can also resolve your delinquency and prevent default, because it results in a new loan and a "fresh start" on your repayment term. Private student loan consolidation and refinancing programs are typically limited to loans that are in good standing, so if your monthly payments on your private loans are becoming unmanageable, it would be prudent to explore private consolidation and refinancing options *before* you start falling behind on payments.

Ultimately, you may have options to prevent default. Talk to your student loan servicer, and if necessary, work with a professional to help figure out what your options are.

Resolving Federal Student Loan Default

Despite your best efforts, it's happened. You've defaulted on your student loans. Perhaps you have already been sent to collections, and a nasty debt collector is hounding you.

You're not alone. The Department of Education estimated that in 2014, *6.8 million* borrowers were in default on their federal student loans. A total of *$95.9 billion* of federal student loans were in default status. That isn't counting all of the borrowers who have defaulted on private student loans (data on private student loan defaults is much less comprehensive).

But don't panic. You may be able to get out of default, especially if your loans are federal. So all is not lost.

Federal Student Loan Rehabilitation

A defaulted federal student loan borrower can individually **rehabilitate** a federal student loan, bringing it out of default via a temporary monthly payment plan. By making nine timely payments over the course of ten months, followed by a transition period in which the loan is placed with a new lender or servicer, a borrower can restore the defaulted federal student loan to good standing.

Rehabilitation plans must be negotiated directly with the applicable loan holder or its contracted debt collection agency. The monthly payment amount for rehabilitation is negotiable to some extent, but borrowers have a right to a "reasonable and affordable" rehabilitation payment based on their income or total financial circumstances. This is usually achieved by using an Income-Based Repayment-type formula to calculate a monthly payment based on the borrower's income and family size, or by conducting a full financial review of the borrower's household income and expenses.

Rehabilitation has a unique credit report advantage: the default notation is completely deleted from your credit report once you have rehabilitated your loan. Other negative information, including the prior delinquencies, may remain in your credit history for some time, but rehabilitation can help to mitigate the worst of the credit impact.

 TIP Once you have rehabilitated a defaulted federal student loan, it cannot be rehabilitated again. It's a one-shot deal.

Federal Direct Loan Consolidation

Consolidation isn't just for borrowers in good standing. It can also help you get out of default. A federal Direct Consolidation loan essentially pays off your defaulted federal loans, just like it would if you were not in default. You would get a single, brand-new federal student loan with one servicing company and one monthly payment, and the new consolidation loan would be in good standing.

Defaulted federal student loan borrowers who are eligible to consolidate do not necessarily have to make any payments to get out of default through Direct loan consolidation, in contrast to rehabilitation. However, you must select an income-driven repayment plan—ICR, IBR, PAYE, or REPAYE—for the new consolidation loan. The process is much faster than rehabilitation but doesn't have the credit report default-deletion advantage.

Federal Student Loan Settlement

It is difficult, but not impossible, to **settle** a defaulted federal student loan for less than the full balance due. These arrangements are unlike most other types of settlements, and they are governed by strict federal guidelines. If you're considering a settlement, be prepared to pay a very sizable portion of the loan balance in a lump-sum payment. There are tax and credit report consequences to settlement as well, so you will want to consult with an attorney and a qualified tax expert before agreeing to anything.

 TIP Federal loan rehabilitation, consolidation, and settlement are complicated programs, and many factors affect a borrower's eligibility. Some options may be better for you than others, depending on your situation. If you are in default and are interested in default resolution, find a student loan attorney to help you navigate these options and advise you properly.

Resolving Private Student Loan Default

Private student loans do not have the same avenues to resolve default as federal student loans do. Private student loan consolidation and refinancing options are already quite limited, and the few private loan consolidation programs that do exist typically do not allow defaulted private loans to be included in a consolidation. Also, private lenders that offer rehabilitation plans are few and far between.

So what does this mean? Once a private student loan is in default, it usually cannot be put back into good standing. Generally, a defaulted private student loan borrower will have four broad options.

Pay in Full

This is the surest way to resolve a private student loan debt, but it is likely not an option for many people (otherwise, you wouldn't have defaulted, right?).

Settle

Settlements resolve the private student loan debt without paying the full balance due. The settlement amount must be negotiated, and will require a payment made via a lump sum or a few limited installments. The exact amount of a settlement will vary depending on the type of loan, the loan holder's settlement criteria, and your own specific circumstances, but private student loan settlements can be much more generous than federal student loan settlements. As with federal loans, there also may be tax and credit report consequences to consider, so you will want to work with an attorney and consult with a tax expert to fully understand your rights and responsibilities.

Ignore

Unlike federal student loans, private lenders are unable to "force" collections through tactics like administrative wage garnishment or offsetting federal benefits, without first obtaining a judgment against you in court. There also is a *statute of limitations* that might apply to private student loans, which means that private lenders have a finite time period within which they must try to collect from you; if they try to collect from you outside of this time period, you may be able to raise the statute of limitations as a defense to a collections action. This limitations period varies considerably from state to state—it's as short as three years in some states and 15 years or longer in others. Ultimately, a private lender could choose to sue you in court before the statute of limitations period has run. If you lose the lawsuit, a judgment will be entered against you, and the private lender could then use power of the courts to enforce the judgment by seizing a portion of your wages or other assets. Thus, there could be significant risk to ignoring the debt.

Make Payments (to You, or to the Loan Holder)

Rather than completely ignore the debt, you can save up for a potential settlement by putting money away every month into an interest-bearing account. That way, if you're sued, you'll have something to negotiate with. In many states, making payments to your lender could restart the clock on the statute-of-limitations period, so saving up by "paying yourself" may help you preserve that defense.

Alternatively, it might be possible to work out a repayment arrangement with the loan holder, either temporarily or on a long-term basis. An installment arrangement would not resolve the default or return the loan to good standing, and it would not guarantee that the lender will not sue you anyway. As mentioned earlier, in many states it could also restart the clock on a statute-of-limitations defense. So this option carries some risk, as well. But it could provide an incentive for the private loan holder not to sue you (after all, it's cheaper for the lender to get free money from you without hiring a law firm to sue you), while you make steady progress toward paying off the loan.

 TIP Your legal rights and options will depend on your specific circumstances, the language in your loan contract, and the law that governs your situation. The ideal strategy for you may not be ideal for someone else. If you have a defaulted student loan, federal or private, you should consult with a qualified attorney to help you navigate the situation.

Conclusions

Given the nasty consequences of default, it should obviously be avoided at all costs. The good news—particularly for federal student loan borrowers—is that default is preventable and, ultimately, curable. However, with the right student loan management plan, you hopefully will never have to worry about defaulting on your student loans. And that gets us to Part 2 of this book.

PART 2

Student Debt Management for Law Students and Attorneys

Now you know everything there is to know about student loans, right? Well, you at least know the basics. Now we're going to apply that basic knowledge to the real world.

Although student debt levels for law students are at record highs, the legal profession is one of the most highly variable in terms of practitioners' income levels. Thus, the student debt repayment strategy for any given attorney must be uniquely tailored to that attorney's professional and financial circumstances. In the following chapters, we'll explore the vastly different strategies and considerations that go into optimizing student loan repayment for the most common attorney career tracks.

For continuity and simplicity, we'll be sticking with the numbers used in the earlier examples and exploring how your strategy will change depending on your job. We'll assume that you are entering repayment—and employment—under similar circumstances as "Sally" did in Part 1 of this book: with $118,700 in federal student loan debt at a 6.8 percent interest rate. You may think that this total loan balance is too high or too low. However, it's pretty close to the average debt burden for private law school graduates during the past several years (and remember, those figures took into account only law school debt, not debt from any prior educational degree programs).

To make things interesting, we're also going to add $35,000 in *private* student loans to this hypothetical student debt portfolio to explore the differences in strategy when you have a combination of federal and private student loans. We'll keep the interest rates the same for all loans, federal and private (6.8 percent).

We'll start with a review of student loan management strategies available while you are still a law student. After all, it's never too early to start being smart about your student debt. From there, we'll explore the differing repayment strategies and considerations for various legal career tracks including the big firm associate, the public interest attorney, the solo practitioner, and others. Read on.

10

Student Loan Management for the Law Student

Before we even get to the exciting world of student loan repayment strategies, it's worth noting that good student loan management begins well before you even graduate. While you're in school, your student loans should be in a deferment status, meaning that no payments are due (go back to Chapter 3 and Chapter 7 if you're not sure how deferment works). But that's not a reason to be asleep at the wheel. Too often, students don't start paying attention to their student debt until right before, or right after, graduation. Don't bury your head in the sand. Be pro-active, and start your student debt management plan *now*.

Minimize Borrowing (to the Extent That You Can)

This may either seem like a no-brainer or a non-starter (law school costs what it costs, and there's nothing we can do about that, right?). But the fact is, under current law, although Stafford loans and Perkins loans are capped, graduate students can borrow *up to the cost of attendance* in federal Graduate PLUS loans. Remember, these loans have some of the highest interest rates out there, often even higher than some private student loans, and they start accruing interest as soon as they are disbursed. There is no interest subsidy. Moreover, a school's "cost of attendance" doesn't just include tuition; it also includes books, fees, and estimated living expenses. I often see graduate students (especially law students) just borrow the maximum allowable amount in Graduate PLUS loans, because they can. *Don't do that.* Just as a small increase in your interest rate can have a big impact on how much you have to repay, a relatively small *decrease* in the amount that you borrow can have a big impact in reducing your overall debt burden, especially since these loans start accruing interest immediately at a fairly high rate.

Think about strategies for reducing the amount that you borrow in Graduate PLUS loans. Be conservative in your initial estimates of how much financial aid you need at the beginning of each academic term or year, and take the time to *budget* your living expenses. Get that smaller, cheaper apartment with four roommates, even if it's not ideal; you have the rest of your life to live in a nicer living situation. Watch your spending. Get a part-time job, or find a summer internship that pays. Be realistic about your needs—don't plan to live on ramen noodles every day for three years—but cut costs wherever you can. None of these steps will make you debt-free, and it's naïve of anyone to suggest otherwise. But if you can cut out a few thousand dollars or more per year in borrowing, it *will* make a difference. And if it turns out that you underborrowed and you cannot make up the difference, you can simply apply midsemester or midyear to take out additional Graduate PLUS loans if necessary. You're not required to borrow everything at the beginning of the school year, but you can't return loans that you've already received. So, be conservative about borrowing. Your future self will thank you.

Monitor Your Student Loans and Maintain Contact with Your Servicers

Don't wait until you get your graduation cap and gown to track down your student loans and figure out what you owe, and who you have to pay. You're going to be too busy taking final exams, looking for a job, and prepping for the bar exam to pay much attention to your student loans, and with all that stress, your mind is going to do everything it can to keep you from adding things to think about. So, make it a habit to know your debt. If you're already in your third year of law school or about to graduate, that's okay—it's not too late. Start now.

Remember, you can get a ton of key information and details about your *federal* student loans via the **National Student Loan Data System (NSLDS)**, an online federal student loan database that aggregates all of the information on every single federal student loan you have ever had: **www.nslds.ed.gov**. Check out this website for key details on your outstanding principal and interest balances, as well as your total federal student loan debt burden. Click on the individual loan detail pages to find out key information on your current federal student loan servicers; these are the companies that are going to bill you, so make sure they have up-to-date contact information for you (including a *non-school-based permanent e-mail address*). All federal student loan servicers have online account access, so be proactive and set up an online account while you are still in school.

As mentioned earlier, there is no equivalent database for private student loans. If you know who your private student loan lender or servicer is, reach out to them and make sure they have up-to-date contact information for you, just like your federal student loan servicers. Your private loan servicers will also likely have online account access, so make things easy for yourself and set up an online account. If you don't know who your private loan holders or servicers are, try pulling your credit report. You are entitled to a free annual credit report from each of the three major bureaus each year (visit www.annualcreditreport.com), so pull your reports and see what outstanding private debts you may have.

Know Your Grace Periods

Remember that after you graduate, many of your student loans will enter a grace period, allowing you to postpone payments for a while (typically six months) while you theoretically search for employment. But not all student loans have grace periods, and not all grace periods last for the same amount of time (refer back to Chapter 2 for more details). Furthermore, grace periods can be used only once during the life of a student loan; this means that if you have student loans from your undergraduate degree or a previous graduate program, you may have already used up some or all of the grace periods for those loans, and they'll enter repayment immediately upon your graduation from law school. The last thing you need is a surprise student loan bill while you're sitting for the bar exam and interviewing for jobs. So contact your loan servicers and find out *exactly* when *each* of your loans enters repayment. If your student loans are all going to be entering repayment at different times, and you don't yet have the capacity to handle the monthly payments, you can put some of your loans that will be entering repayment sooner into a brief temporary deferment or forbearance to buy yourself a few months and line everything up. Talk to your loan servicer about your options.

Prepare for Repayment

Whether you like it or not, your loans *will* enter repayment at some point after you graduate, and you want to be prepared.

- If you have federal student loans with multiple loan servicers, or you have a mix of Direct and non-Direct federal student loans, consider consolidating your loans via the federal Direct Consolidation loan program to simplify repayment and maximize your eligibility for available repayment and forgiveness programs. You cannot consolidate until your loans are no longer in an in-school deferment (although you *can* consolidate during your grace periods).
- If you don't yet have a job lined up, consider an *income-driven repayment plan* for your federal student loans rather than a deferment or forbearance; $0 in income means $0/month in payments under those plans, so you won't have to pay anything; but, unlike a deferment or forbearance, you're making progress toward loan forgiveness while in an income-driven plan, even if your calculated monthly payment is $0. For private student loans (which typically do not have income-driven repayment plan options), ride out your grace periods, and request a deferment or forbearance only if you absolutely have to; private student loan payment postponement options are usually very limited.

- If you do have employment lined up right after graduation, consider making voluntary payments before your grace periods end. You don't *have* to do this, and if your projected employment does not have a particularly high salary, you probably shouldn't. Still, getting a head start on your repayment means that less interest will accrue over the life of the loan, and that's less money that you have to pay back.

Employing these strategies may make the transition from student life to professional life significantly easier. And when you're already fully loaded on stress from job searching and bar exam studying, you will appreciate *not* having to worry about something.

11

Student Loan Management for the Big Firm and Corporate Attorney

Average starting salaries for first-year associates at the nation's top law firms can be $160,000 per year or higher—and that's just for the first year. In-house counsel positions also typically provide six-figure salaries. Given these numbers, paying off your student loans should be fairly easy and straightforward, right? Well, not exactly. Here's what you should be thinking about.

Select a Level, Balance-Based Repayment Plan

Given our hypothetical federal loan balance of $118,700 and the income ranges we're talking about for corporate and big firm attorneys, there's no real reason to select an income-driven repayment plan. You can likely afford the monthly payments under available balance-based plans, and there's no need to put yourself through the annual bureaucratic process of recalculating your monthly payments under the income-driven plans. But which balance-based plan is right for you?

I recommend against graduated repayment plans in general, but especially for attorneys going into Big Law. Selecting a repayment plan that sets you up for larger and larger payments over time is a rather risky endeavor for any profession because it assumes that your income will continue to increase to compensate for the larger payments. But keep in mind how the Big Law associate system tends to work: a large first-year associate class comes in, and then each year, that class dwindles down as attorneys leave (voluntarily or involuntarily) for any number of positions in a variety of fields. When attorneys leave a Big Law job for another gig—whether it's for a smaller firm, a nonprofit organization, or a company—they often take a pay cut. Furthermore, your monthly payments under a graduated repayment plan are as low as they can possibly be in the early years and will mostly be going toward interest. With a federal loan balance of $118,700 at a 6.8 percent interest rate, you're accruing interest at the rate of approximately **$672 per month**. Initial payments under the graduated plans are only marginally higher than this. Thus, if you start out on a graduated plan and then leave the high-paying world of Big Law or corporate law after a few years, you may be surprised to see that you've made thousands of dollars in payments but barely a dent in your loan balance.

Instead, choose a level balance-based repayment plan to maximize these high-income earning years and pay down your balance: either the 10-year plan, the 25-year plan, or the 30-year plan (available for Direct Consolidation loans with balances in excess of $60,000). Under any of these plans, you're making progress toward loan payoff. Your monthly payments will obviously be vastly different depending on the repayment term that you choose; continuing with our $118,700 figure at a 6.8 percent rate, you'll pay **$1,370** per month for the 10-year level plan, but only **$825** per month under the 25-year level plan. If you're the type of person who wants to prioritize relatively rapid loan payoff (and you can afford it), select the 10-year plan. If you want more flexibility with a lower minimum monthly payment, go with the 25-year plan, or consolidate to get on the 30-year plan. It really comes down to your priorities, your discipline, and your budget. As with any federal student loan repayment plan, there's no penalty for making monthly payments *higher* than your minimums, so if you have a particularly good month, you can always pay more. Remember, because of how interest accrues, the more quickly you pay down that principal, the less money you'll pay in total over time.

Just keep in mind that you're going to have that private student loan to deal with as well—and you're not going to have much of a selection of repayment plan options. With a balance of $35,000 and an interest rate of 6.8 percent, you'll have a monthly payment of more than **$245** for a 25-year repayment term (which is fairly typical for private student loans). So factor that additional payment into whatever payment plan you select for your federal loans.

Targeted Accelerated Repayment or Payoff

In addition to providing you with the flexibility to select a balance-based repayment plan that best suits your needs and priorities, your high income as a big firm associate or corporate attorney may give you the ability to select certain student loans to voluntarily repay faster than other loans. There are several strategies that you can consider.

Target Your Private Loans

Private student loans tend to have far fewer repayment options and much less flexibility in times of economic difficulty as compared to their federal counterparts. If you're on a balance-based repayment plan for your federal student loans and you fall on hard times, or you choose to leave your high-paying job for something more modest, you can always go into an income-driven repayment plan or opt into the generous deferment and forbearance programs available to federal student loan borrowers. These safety nets are generally either quite limited or completely nonexistent in the private loan realm. Although this may not be a problem for you now while things are good, it could be a problem for you in the future. By targeting your private student loans for rapid payoff (perhaps by selecting a longer repayment term for your federal student loans, and then paying as much as you can—higher than your minimums—for your private loans), you can reduce this risk significantly.

Target Your Higher-Interest-Rate Loans

Alternatively, rather than basing your payoff acceleration priorities on the *type* of loan, you can take a purely financial approach and target your highest-interest loans. Remember from Chapter 5 how significant one or two interest rate points can be in terms of how effective your monthly payments are, and how much you'll repay over the course of a repayment term. By paying off your highest-interest loans as quickly as possible, you can reduce the total amount you'll pay. These high-interest loans *may* be your private loans (since private loans tend to have high interest rates), but they might instead be your federal Graduate PLUS loans, which tend to have interest rates of at least 7 percent or 8 percent. Check with your loan servicer to get comprehensive information on your interest rates. If it turns out that you have high-interest federal loans that you want to target for accelerated payoff, you'll want to exclude them from any consolidation (otherwise they will cease to be identifiable individual loans).

Target Your Lower-Balance Loans

A final approach would be to focus on paying off one loan at a time in its entirety, starting with the loans with the smallest balances. This tends to be most effective for borrowers who have multiple private student loans with multiple lenders (and correspondingly multiple monthly payments). Each time you eliminate one of your loans, you're eliminating its associated monthly payment obligation, freeing up additional resources to target the next-smallest loan in your portfolio. From a purely financial perspective, paying off your smallest loans first is not usually the most advantageous move unless your smallest loans also have the highest interest rates. Still, completing repayment on a loan can be an enormous weight off your shoulders, even if it's your smallest loan. As a side benefit, each loan you fully repay reduces the number of accounts you have to check, and the amount of time you have to dedicate to monitoring your loan repayments in the future. For an overworked associate at a big law firm, the emotional relief and time savings may be well worth the small cost.

Loan Refinancing

While it is not possible right now to refinance federal student loans at a lower interest rate within the federal student loan system, there are a growing number of private student loan refinancing and consolidation programs through which borrowers can refinance their private student loans, their federal student loans, or both. The programs that offer the most attractive repayment plan terms and interest rates tend to be geared toward very high-income earners with excellent credit. For attorneys, that combination of qualities is likely going to be found most in the Big Law and corporate law fields. Given the high interest rates of Graduate PLUS loans and many private student loans, refinancing is certainly something to consider. However, when looking into specific refinancing options, especially if you're including some or all of your federal loans, be sure that you're thinking about the big picture.

What's the Interest Rate?

An interest rate reduction is, obviously, one of the primary reasons to refinance. But don't just look at a number and assume that you're getting a better deal. For example, is the interest rate fixed, or is it variable? If it's variable, how is the interest rate calculated? Is it capped? How high can the interest rate go? These are critical questions when examining a private student loan refinancing program. A three-point interest rate reduction is not particularly helpful if it's going to turn into a five-point interest rate increase in a few years.

What's the Repayment Term and the Monthly Payment?

It's important to fully understand what your monthly payments are going to look like. If you refinance your entire student loan portfolio and keep the same loan repayment term but lower your interest rate, you should see a drop in your monthly payment, which is great. But remember that if you're refinancing federal student loans, you're losing out on the safety net of the income-driven repayment plans, should you experience a drop in income in the future. So take a long, hard look at that monthly payment and ask yourself if you think you'll be in a position to make those payments five, 10, or 20 years from now, depending on the loan term. If you don't see yourself staying in a high-paying big firm or corporate position for the indefinite future, or you're not sure, be careful.

Are There Origination Fees?

Some private student loan refinancing programs charge quite hefty *origination fees* as a percentage of the total loan balance that you're refinancing. Those fees get tacked onto the refinanced loan and it's something you have to repay. Sometimes, these origination fees can negate a good chunk of the savings you might be getting through an interest rate reduction, in which case what's the point of refinancing? Read the fine print carefully, and do some calculations to compare those costs to any potential savings.

Do the Loan Terms Provide Flexibility?

I may sound like a broken record here, but private student loans just do not have the same flexible options if you fall on hard times, as compared to federal student loans. Still, some programs are better than others, particularly when it comes to private student loan refinancing programs. Check out the loan terms to see what happens if you lose your job, get sick, or experience some other type of personal or financial hardship. Are there deferment or forbearance options? If so, how much? Are there options to reduce your monthly payments? If so, for how long? If the refinanced loan requires a cosigner, is there a mechanism to get the cosigner released?

It's always hard to predict the future, especially when things are going well, but don't let a lower interest rate or lower monthly payment be the only factors when choosing what refinancing program is best for you—or whether to refinance at all.

12

Student Loan Management for the Government and Nonprofit Attorney

While big firm associates and corporate in-house counsel are raking in the money with six-figure salaries, government and nonprofit sector attorneys (including judicial clerks) are on the complete opposite end of the attorney income spectrum, with annual salaries that are a fraction of those of their corporate and big firm counterparts. Here in Massachusetts where I practice, the starting salaries for public defenders, assistant district attorneys, and civil legal service attorneys are under $45,000. Elsewhere, it's not much better.

Given this wide disparity in income, you might think that if you're a government or nonprofit attorney, there is no possible way to manage our hypothetical student loan debt portfolio totaling more than $150,000 in federal and private loans. That's not necessarily the case, however. You're just going to have a much different repayment approach.

Income-Driven Repayment

Income-driven repayment programs might be the single most important option available to government and nonprofit attorneys because they will allow you to stay in good standing on your loans (at least the federal ones) even with a low income. For a single borrower making $45,000 per year, your monthly income-driven payment will be in the $230 to $345 range, depending on the plan you select (or the best plan you are eligible for). Be sure to review the eligibility requirements for each of the income-driven plans to see which one is the best plan for you; remember that for some of the plans, you may have to *consolidate* your federal loans through the federal Direct consolidation loan program if you have a mix of FFEL and Direct loans. Alternatively, the standardized income-driven repayment plan application gives you the option to have your loan servicer review your loan portfolio and determine the plan that will give you the lowest monthly payment.

The most important thing to remember when it comes to income-driven repayment is the requirement to recertify your income every 12 months to remain in the program. If you fail to recertify your income, you can be dropped from income-driven repayment and placed on a Standard repayment plan; furthermore, any outstanding interest will be capitalized, leading to compound interest accrual. Loan servicers are supposed to notify borrowers 60 to 90 days in advance of the recertification deadline, but a prudent borrower in income-driven repayment would mark her calendar for nine months after she enters an income-driven repayment plan and proactively contact her loan servicer for instructions on recertification.

Perkins Loan Cancellation

As discussed in Chapter 8, federal Perkins loans are special and have their own provisions allowing for full or partial cancellation if you work in certain specialized professions. The key professions for attorneys are *public defenders* and *prosecuting attorneys* (such as assistant district attorneys and assistant attorneys general). If you work in these professions, you can get a portion of your Perkins loans canceled each year that you remain in qualifying employment. You can ultimately get your full Perkins loan balance forgiven after five years of service, without ever having to repay a dime. Just be very careful: if you *consolidate* your Perkins loans with your other federal loans, you will not be able to obtain these benefits. There is no way to un-consolidate a loan.

Public Service Loan Forgiveness

Public Service Loan Forgiveness (PSLF) is a critical incentive for attorneys working for government or in the nonprofit sector. Although PSLF does not change your monthly payment amount, it does allow attorneys working in public service to get their loans forgiven after 120 qualifying payments have been made on Direct-program loans under income-driven repayment plans. Remember the key requirements of the program:

- Only Direct loans are eligible. Thus, if you have a mix of FFEL and Direct loans, you may need to consolidate through the Direct consolidation program. If you have Perkins loans, consider whether to include them in the consolidation loan based on your specific profession. If they are excluded from a consolidation and they are not eligible for profession-based cancellation, you'll have to make separate and additional monthly payments on them, and there's no income-driven repayment for Perkins loans.

- Only payments made under income-driven repayment plans (or the 10-year Standard plan) qualify. This may be a no-brainer for public service attorneys, but it's a reason to be *in repayment*, as opposed to deferment or forbearance. *Deferment and forbearance do not count toward PSLF, even if you are making voluntary payments.*

- You must be considered a full-time employee by your employer, *and* you must work at least 30 hours per week. That means that if you work 32 hours per week but your employer considers you part-time, you may not qualify. However, if you have multiple part-time public service jobs that add up to at least 30 hours per week, taken together this should be considered qualifying employment.

- Remember, think of PSLF as a 120-payment program, not necessarily a 10-year program. You *can* get your loans forgiven after 10 years if you remain in public service continuously and never miss a payment. But PSLF also allows you to work in the private sector, and then come back into public service later in your career. Your prior payments will still count toward the 120 payments required to obtain forgiveness.

Many public service positions will qualify for PSLF, but not all of them. Employment in any branch of government (executive, legislative, judicial), at any level (municipal, county, state, federal) will qualify. This also includes public schools and the military—so, for example, attorneys working in the U.S. Army JAG Corps would qualify. Employment for most domestic nonprofit organizations will qualify if the employer is a registered 501(c)(3) nonprofit organization; this includes most nonprofit colleges and universities, legal services organizations, professional associations (including bar associations), and legal education organizations. However, employment in partisan political organizations, labor unions, and international nongovernmental organizations generally does not count, and non-501(c)(3) nonprofit organizations qualify only if they engage in specific types of public service work (i.e., public health or legal services). If you're not sure if your employment qualifies, you can visit the website of FedLoan Servicing (www.myfedloan.org), the U.S. Department of Education loan servicer that handles public service borrowers, to access its resources on PSLF employment.

If your employment does qualify for PSLF, even 10 years is a long time to wait, however. Borrowers who want to officially track their payments can do so by completing the Public Service Loan Forgiveness Program Employment Certification form, available through FedLoan Servicing (www.myfedloan.org). After you submit it with your employer's signature, the U.S. Department of Education will issue you a letter providing you with the number of qualifying payments you have made thus far, the number of qualifying payments remaining, and the anticipated date that your loans will be forgiven. While you are not required to complete this form, the U.S. Department of Education recommends that you submit this form annually and whenever you separate from an employer.

Loan Repayment Assistance Programs

Many law schools have loan repayment assistance programs (LRAPs), through which they provide financial assistance to graduates to help them repay their student loans. Most LRAPs are specifically profession-dependent, meaning that borrowers are eligible only if they work in certain professions (usually public interest jobs). LRAPs typically work by providing annual or semiannual lump-sum payments to borrowers that can be used toward their student loan obligations. Depending on the specific program, LRAPs may act essentially as a gift. For other programs, the LRAP payments may start off as a "loan" that you can use to pay your student loan bills (federal or private), and then—as long as you remain eligible for the program—the "loan" converts to a grant that you never have to repay. If you're working as a government or nonprofit attorney, LRAPs can be a lifesaver. Some programs will completely cover your monthly payment obligations, or at least a good chunk of them.

Check with your school's financial aid office to see what your school offers and what the eligibility requirements are. Most schools have strict application deadlines, and if you miss them, you're out of luck. Just like annual recertification for income-driven repayment, mark your calendar for your school's LRAP application deadline and be sure to *get it done.* An LRAP award may be critical to staying afloat on a low salary with six figures of student loan debt dragging you down.

Private Student Loan Management

The most difficult part of managing your student loans while on a public service salary will be your private loans. If you're lucky, you won't have any, since federal Graduate PLUS loans should cover the cost of a law school education without the need for private funding (although this was not always the case). But you may have private student loans, either from a prior degree, a Bar Study financing program, or both. To use our ongoing hypothetical loan portfolio, if you have $35,000 in private student loans at a 6.8 percent interest rate, your monthly payments may be in excess of $245, assuming a 20- or 25-year repayment term. This payment will be an additional obligation on top of your federal student loan payment.

There is no magic bullet for managing your private student loans on a low public service salary. You cannot consolidate private student loans into the federal student loan system to take advantage of income-driven repayment and loan forgiveness, and you're unlikely to be able to refinance the private loan at a lower rate, given the eligibility criteria for many private refinancing programs, which often require high levels of income. Instead, your best bet is to take advantage of the programs and tools that are available to you to manage your federal loans: income-driven repayment, loan cancellation and forgiveness, and LRAP programs. Get your federal student loan payments as low as they can be, try to get the biggest LRAP award that you can get, and budget wisely. It will be challenging, but not impossible, to keep a private student loan in good standing while working as a public service attorney.

13

Student Loan Management for the Small and Medium Firm Attorney

The vast majority of practicing attorneys work in small and medium-size firms. In some ways, the small and medium firm attorneys have it the toughest in terms of managing their student loans and optimizing repayment. Big firm and corporate lawyers have the large salaries that give them the flexibility to broadly pay down their student loans and to target certain aspects of their student debt portfolio for more rapid payoff. Attorneys working in public service certainly don't have that financial flexibility, but they have access to numerous programs that can make managing large student debt balances completely doable, with loan cancellation and forgiveness as ultimate safety nets for balances that could otherwise never be repaid in full. But the small and medium firm attorneys are stuck in the middle. Their salaries are usually higher than those of their colleagues working in the public and nonprofit sectors, but significantly less than their large firm and corporate counterparts. Meanwhile, they may not have access to the broad array of loan forgiveness and LRAP programs, which are typically geared toward people working in public service.

So, how should you manage your student loans if you work for a small or medium firm? The answers will largely depend on your student loan portfolio, your income, your family, your priorities, and your budget, but ultimately it boils down to *being strategic*.

Carefully Choose Your Repayment Plan

We're going to continue with our student debt portfolio example of $118,700 in total federal student loan debt, plus an additional $35,000 in private student loan debt, all at a 6.8 percent interest rate. Before we even start taking a close look at repayment plans, there are a few important considerations to keep in mind.

Private Student Loan

You will likely have no choice regarding your private student loan repayment. For our purposes, we're going to assume that you have a 25-year repayment term, and that's it. So, to figure out what *federal* student loan repayment plan is the best fit for you, you first have to approach the private student loan monthly payment of $245 as a given. You're paying that no matter what, and you must factor that into your monthly budget. Choose your federal student loan repayment plan based on what you can afford with your remaining income.

Avoid Negative Amortization (If You Can)

For borrowers with low incomes and high federal student loan debt balances on income-driven repayment plans, negative amortization may be unavoidable. For middle- and higher-income earners, though, the repayment plan options may straddle both sides of the negative amortization line. In other words, you may have access to some income-driven repayment plans that allow you to pay less than your monthly interest accrual, while other repayment plans (income-driven and balance-based) may allow you to pay more. *If it's possible for you,* you should try to avoid negative amortization for your federal student loans. Why? Because your income is likely going to rise over time, even if only gradually, and if you are subsequently able to afford payments that cover all of your monthly interest accrual and some principal, you'll have a lot more to repay if you've been negatively amortizing for years. For our hypothetical federal loan balance of $118,700, interest is accruing at the rate of approximately **$672 per month**. Remember that number.

Family Size Matters

For the income-driven repayment plans, remember that the formulas don't just take into account your income: they also take into account your family size. Your monthly payments will be lower if you're financially supporting several people in your household than if you're single. This may be significant for borrowers who simply need to be on the cheapest possible payment plan, regardless of the potential interest consequences.

With all this in mind, let's take a look at some examples. Each of the three attorneys in the following scenario has a different annual income. The level balance-based plans will obviously be the same in all three examples, but the income-driven options will change, including when family size is taken into consideration.

Note that I am *not* including examples for the graduated balance-based repayment plans, as I generally think that these are poor repayment plan choices for attorneys working in small and medium firms. Your income would have to rise at a pretty unreasonable rate to keep up with the periodic increases in monthly payments under those plans. Better to go with a predictable, level repayment plan or, if you can't afford that, one that's based on your income and family size.

I am also not including the Income-Contingent Repayment (ICR) plan in these examples. For the below borrowers, at least one of the balance-based plans will likely be cheaper than the ICR plan, and if you can't afford any of the balance-based plans, you're going to want to select either the Income-Based Repayment (IBR) plan or the Pay As You Earn (PAYE) plan, both of which are cheaper than ICR.

Example 1: Approximate Monthly Payments with an Adjusted Gross Income of $55,000:

- Level 10-year plan: $1,380
- Level 25-year plan: $835
- Level 30-year plan: $785
- IBR (family size of 1): $470
- PAYE (family size of 1): $310
- IBR (family size of 4): $235
- PAYE (family size of 4): $155

In this example, all of the income-driven repayment plan options are going to be cheaper than the balance-based options—significantly cheaper, in fact. However, under all of the income-driven plans, you're going to experience negative amortization, as your monthly payment is less than the amount of interest that is accruing on your loans each month. Thus, you're going to have to take a close look at your budget, see what you can reasonably afford per month, and weigh the benefits of a lower payment against the potential risks of negative amortization.

Example 2: Approximate Monthly Payments with an Adjusted Gross Income of $70,000:

- Level 10-year plan: $1,380
- Level 25-year plan: $835
- Level 30-year plan: $785
- IBR (family size of 1): $655
- PAYE (family size of 1): $440
- IBR (family size of 4): $420
- PAYE (family size of 4): $280

In this example, your monthly payments under the income-driven repayment plans are also all cheaper than the balance-based options, but the disparity is less significant, especially if you are single with no dependents. The IBR payment for a single borrower at this income level is not much less than the monthly payment under the 30-year payment plan available for Direct consolidation loans. Importantly, though, that is the difference between being on a plan that will cause negative amortization and being on a plan that will not. Again, you'll have to take a close look at your budget (don't forget about that private loan) and weigh the benefits and pitfalls of each option.

Example 3: Approximate Monthly Payments with an Adjusted Gross Income of $90,000:

- Level 10-year plan: $1,380
- Level 25-year plan: $835
- Level 30-year plan: $785
- IBR (family size of 1): $905
- PAYE (family size of 1): $605
- IBR (family size of 4): $670
- PAYE (family size of 4): $450

This is where things start to get interesting. In this example, monthly payments for both the 25-year and 30-year level plans are actually *cheaper* than the monthly payment for the single borrower on IBR. Thus, for that borrower, it may make more sense to just select one of those balance-based plans, where you know you are paying off both principal and interest—and because there's no penalty for paying more than your minimums, you can decide on a month-to-month basis whether to allocate more money to your loans. In contrast, the borrower who selects PAYE and the borrower with a family size of four are both still going to save money—and experience at least *some* negative amortization—on an income-driven repayment plan. They'll have to go through the same budgetary review and prioritization exercise as the borrowers in the prior lower-income examples.

Be Smart About Targeted Payoff

Having a lower annual income than big firm and corporate attorneys means you may have relatively less money to work with, but it doesn't mean you won't have the opportunity to target certain loans within your debt portfolio for more rapid payoff. Many small and medium law firms offer bonuses to their associates. You may have a particularly strong year with new client acquisition, or you may win a big contingency fee case. Some way or another, you may find yourself with some extra cash.

If this happens to you, don't just throw it at your student loans. Be smart about it. Put that extra income in the context of your overall financial goals and budgetary needs. If it does make sense to make an extra lump-sum payment toward your student loans, target your private student loan first. While the big firm attorneys have more consistently high income that gives them some flexibility in allocating extra earnings toward their debt portfolio, for small and medium firm attorneys, the private student loan in our hypothetical example is the biggest deadweight. It likely has the worst terms and conditions, and it requires an extra monthly payment that you want to get rid of as soon as possible to free up some cash resources. If you put the extra money toward your federal student loans, you may put a dent in your balance and accelerate the eventual payoff of those loans, but your monthly payments won't change. Eliminating the private student loan will free up resources so you can pay down the federal student loans more quickly.

If you don't have private student loans and want to be able to target higher-interest federal student loans for accelerated payoff, remember to exclude those higher-interest-rate loans from any consolidation.

Targeted Refinancing

Having a lower salary does not mean you cannot refinance your loans, but it does mean you'll have to be more strategic about it. Because of your lower salary, it's less likely that private student loan refinancers will allow you to refinance your entire loan portfolio (and if they do, you might not get much of an interest rate reduction). Even if it's possible, however, given your relatively lower salary compared to the highest-earning attorneys, it may not be the wisest decision to refinance *all* of your student loans. Remember, refinancing your federal student loans through a private loan refinancing vehicle is a one-way street out of the federal student loan safety net programs, including income-driven repayment and loan forgiveness.

As with targeted payoff, your first refinancing goal should be that private student loan. If you can refinance your private 6.8 percent, $35,000 private loan and get a 4.5 percent interest rate on the same repayment term, you can lower your monthly payment to less than $200/month, even with a 3 percent origination fee. That may make a significant difference in your monthly budget, and it will save you $500 to $600 per year. Or you could refinance the loan at a lower rate and *shorten* the repayment term, keeping the same monthly payment but paying the loan off sooner. This will save you money in terms of the total amount you pay over the repayment term.

If you have no private student loans to refinance, you can consider refinancing some of your highest-interest federal student loans. Just bear in mind what you're giving up in terms of federal student loan programs: generous deferment and forbearance options, long-term income-driven repayment plans, and various loan forgiveness programs that are limited to federal student loan borrowers.

14

Student Loan Management for the Solo Practitioner

More attorneys are starting their own practices early in their careers than ever before.[1] The biggest challenge for solo practitioners when it comes to student loan management, and financial management in general, is unpredictability. Your income may be quite low when you're first starting out, and there's no way to know when you'll start turning a profit. Even when you start earning a decent living, you may experience wild fluctuations in income from month to month or from year to year. But student loan repayment obligations operate on a regular monthly payment cycle. Lenders and servicers don't necessarily take into account the fact that your income may never be exactly the same in any given week, month, or year. So, what does the solo practitioner do to best manage his or her student loans?

Beware of Deferment and Forbearance

Given the financial uncertainties of solo practice, especially when you're first starting out, it may be tempting to just put all of your loans into a deferment and forbearance to postpone your payment obligations. Out of sight, out of mind, as they say. And you might actually be in a financial hardship if you're not earning enough money to meet your basic needs—that's a legitimate basis for requesting a postponement for your student loan payments. But deferment and forbearance may not be the best strategy.

Remember, during deferment and forbearance, interest is continuing to accrue on all of your loans, and you cannot make any progress toward loan forgiveness under any available program. Furthermore, nearly all deferment and forbearance options are time-limited. Although the federal programs are far more generous than their private counterparts, all deferments and forbearances will eventually end, and you'll have no choice but to enter repayment—except now that you've

---

1 *See* Elizabeth Olson, *Burdened with Debt, Law School Graduates Struggle in Job Market*, The New York Times, April 26, 2015.

used up all your deferment and forbearance options, you will have absolutely no margin for error should you experience another economic hardship.

For your private student loans, make your monthly payments if you can, especially if you can manage your federal student loans by making marginal monthly payments (more on that later). If you absolutely cannot afford your private student loan payments, then contact your servicer to determine your options. You may be able to get on a temporary reduced payment plan or postpone your payments through forbearance. This may buy you a little time, but try to avoid using up all of your options at the outset.

For your federal student loans, income-driven repayment may be the way to go.

Income-Driven Repayment for the Solo Practitioner

Without a steady, predictable, documented income, many solos think that there's no way an income-driven repayment plan can work for them. That's simply not the case. You just have to understand your options.

Documenting Your Income

For most people on an income-driven repayment plan, the easiest way to provide your loan servicer with proof of your income is to produce a copy of your tax return or a pay stub. But as a solo practitioner, you don't have a pay stub, and your most recently filed tax return may not always reflect the income you are currently earning when it is time to send in your documentation.

Federal loan servicers allow borrowers applying or recertifying for income-driven repayment plans to submit *alternative documentation of income* when traditional forms of income documentation are not available. This can be a simple, self-certifying signed statement providing your gross income per time period (e.g., $2,000 per month) and a brief explanation as to where that income comes from, coupled with proof of your self-employment such as a business certificate or federal employer identification number. For solo practitioners who are just establishing their practices, your monthly income may be negligible; a gross income of less than $18,000 per year (or $1,500/month) would result in a $0/month payment under the IBR and PAYE plans, which would avoid the need for any deferment or forbearance while putting you on track for loan forgiveness (remember, even $0/month "payments" count toward 25-year and 20-year loan forgiveness under IBR and PAYE, respectively). For better established solo practitioners, the self-certifying statement can provide a much-needed alternative method of obtaining a reasonable monthly payment if your tax return does not reflect what you're currently earning (for example, if last year's income as reported on your tax return was artificially inflated by a one-time big win on a contingency-fee case). Contact your loan servicer to get more information on specific requirements for alternative documentation of income, such as self-certifying statements.

Recalculating Your Monthly Payment

To stay in an income-driven repayment plan, you must recertify your income and reapply for the plan every 12 months. This works just fine for borrowers who earn steady, predictable incomes—but for solo practitioners, this can be disastrous. If your current monthly payment is based on income documentation that you sent six or seven months ago when business was good, and you're now in a months-long rut, it may not be possible for you to make your payments for the full 12-month period.

Luckily, income-driven repayment plans provide borrowers with the right to request a *recalculation* of their monthly payments at any time if their circumstances change. If your current monthly payment is based on a gross monthly income of $7,500 per month ($90,000 per year), but during the past few months you've been scraping by earning just $2,000 per month, you probably are going to have a tough time keeping up with your IBR payments of $905/month based on that earlier, higher figure. You can contact your loan servicer and submit an application to request that your servicer recalculate your payment based on your changed circumstances. That would bring your monthly payment down to $55/month—a huge difference.

Switching Repayment Plans

Remember that you are not locked in to *any* repayment plan. Thus, for more-established solo practitioners who may be earning a more consistent steady income, a balance-based repayment plan might just make the most sense. With a balance-based plan, you would have a predictable monthly payment amount without having to deal with the income-driven repayment applications or figuring out how to best document your income. If your circumstances change, however, and your income drops, you can always apply for an income-driven repayment plan. You can also switch out of an income-driven repayment plan and go back into a balance-based plan (there are no limitations on the number of times a borrower can switch back and forth between an income-driven repayment plan and a balance-based repayment plan). Just keep in mind that if you have experienced negative amortization during the income-based repayment period, any outstanding interest will be capitalized when you leave income-driven repayment and go onto a balance-based plan.

Handling Windfalls

Unpredictable income isn't always a bad thing. As a solo practitioner, you may have a particularly strong month or year. If you take some cases on a contingency-fee basis, you may get a substantial financial award at various sporadic points during your career. Avoid the temptation to just throw money at your student loans, however. As with all of the prior career tracks we've discussed, you want to be strategic about what you do with this extra cash.

Emergency Fund

Any good financial planner will tell you that you should have an emergency fund: a savings account that can cover at least three to six months of expenses if something bad or unexpected occurs. An emergency fund is particularly important for solo practitioners because it doesn't take a catastrophic event (such as an injury or illness) to put you in a financial bind. Your business may just take a downturn for a few months. It happens, and in fact it probably *will* happen to you at some point—more than once. If you have an emergency fund built up to carry you through these ruts, then you can weather these business downturns. Income-driven repayment is great for your federal student loans, but it doesn't exist for your private loans, or for most other recurring financial obligations. If you don't have a sufficient emergency fund and you get a major inflow of revenue, don't throw the money at your student loans; build, maintain, and replenish your emergency fund first.

Prioritize Your Private Student Loans for Payoff

If you've got your emergency fund covered, then you can turn to your private student loans when you get that extra influx of cash. The burden of the private student loan transcends all careers, within the legal field and outside of it. That monthly payment is a problem that you want to eliminate, and given the relatively modest size of the private student loan in our ongoing hypothetical example, it should be doable for you to chip away at that balance. Even if it means that you pay just a few thousand dollars on top of your regular monthly payments every year, you'll repay that loan in full far sooner than if you just made the minimum payments for the full repayment term.

Balance Accelerated Federal Student Loan Payment with Your Other Goals and Needs

If you are in the enviable position of having established a robust emergency fund, and you've paid off all of your private student loans, your solo practice must be doing pretty well, and you should feel good. But now the question becomes, what do you do with significant extra cash? Should you now prioritize the accelerated payoff of your federal student loans? This is a more complex and nuanced question for the solo practitioner than for people in other careers. As a solo practitioner, you have certain considerations that other attorneys do not have in their jobs; for example, you have to save for retirement, and you don't exactly have an "employer match" program, do you? You may also want to consider growing and expanding your practice—an endeavor that may yield higher income later, but may require some initial upfront spending, along with a healthy amount of financial risk-taking. Thus, although accelerating the payoff of federal student loans may make sense for some established solo practitioners, it may not make as much sense for others. Decisions about what to do with extra revenue in such circumstances should be made in conjunction with careful financial and business planning, preferably with an objective outside professional.

15

Student Loan Management for the Contract Attorney

Just as the solo practitioner must deal with shifting and unpredictable income, which can make management of student loans seem nearly impossible, so must contract attorneys. But while solo practitioners at least have the certainty of ongoing employment as long as they want it (at least in theory), contract attorneys do not. Projects may come and go, last for varying periods of time, and have significantly different payment structures. There may be gaps in contract employment or projects, which can make student loan management particularly tricky. Still, there are strategies the contract attorney can employ to make things manageable.

Income-Driven Repayment

As with the solo practitioner, income-driven repayment is likely going to be the way to go. You'll want to think about the best way to document your income so that it most accurately reflects what you are currently earning. If that's not your tax return, remember that you can provide *alternative documentation of income*, as described in Chapter 14. For contract attorneys, this may be your current employment contract that describes your pay structure, or an actual pay stub if you are issued regular paychecks. You can also ask the entity that is contracting you to write a letter specifying how much you are paid during a given pay period. Like the solo practitioner, you can also request a *recalculation* of your monthly payment amount under any income-driven plan if your circumstances change. So, if you're working a 6-month contract that pays $4,000/month, and that's the basis for your income-driven monthly payment, you can request that your payment amount be recalculated if you then switch to a new contract that pays only $2,000/month.

There are some problems with income-driven repayment that are unique to contract attorneys, however. Many entities employing attorneys as contractors do not pay benefits, and income-driven repayment plans do not take into account your expenses. Therefore, budgeting for monthly student loan payments may be particularly challenging when you work as a contract attorney. Contractors should also be careful about the form of income documentation that they use: you need to be truthful and accurate, but you also don't want to end up with a higher payment than you may otherwise need to have. For instance, many contract attorneys are considered "independent contractors" and are thus not issued regular paychecks with payroll deductions; these attorneys may be issued a Form 1099 at the end of the year showing their total earnings. Because the Form 1099 shows total gross earnings, unadjusted and before any itemized deductions, the contract attorney should consider whether or not using the Form 1099 as documentation of income would be preferable to using his or her tax return. Remember that if you use your tax return, the key figure that your servicer will examine is the adjusted gross income, which is inherently *adjusted* to account for certain pretax deductions and adjustments. Thus, some contract attorneys may be better off using their tax return, rather than the Form 1099 or a pay stub that has no payroll deductions.

Dealing with Gaps in Employment

As with the solo practitioner, contract attorneys should resist the temptation to go into deferment or forbearance when there are gaps in earnings between employment contracts. Remember, during deferment and forbearance, interest is continuing to accrue on all of your loans, and you cannot make any progress toward loan forgiveness under any available program. Also, as mentioned before, deferment and forbearance options are time-limited, so if you use up all of your available deferment and forbearance options, you'll eventually be in a situation where you will have no margin of error should you ever encounter a true emergency. Furthermore, if you've been on an income-driven repayment plan that has resulted in negative amortization, leaving that plan and going into a hardship forbearance can result in any outstanding interest being capitalized—and we already know the dangers of that.

Rather than go into deferment or forbearance when you're between contracts, the better route would be to switch to an income-driven repayment plan if you're not already on one, or request a recalculation of your income-driven monthly payments. If you are earning no income, then your monthly payment will be $0/month under all of these plans, for up to 12 months. This will provide the exact same relief as a deferment or forbearance, but it keeps you on track for loan forgiveness, doesn't result in interest capitalization, and doesn't eat into your deferment and forbearance options, which really should be used only in times of a true, and temporary, emergency. If your circumstances change again, you can request yet another recalculation of your monthly payments. If they don't, and your gap in employment is significant, you'll simply document that your income is still $0 when it is time to recertify your income-driven repayment plan, and your payments will stay at $0/month for the next cycle.

Loan Forgiveness Limitations

Contract attorneys on income-driven repayment plans can make progress toward eventual loan forgiveness (20 or 25 years, depending on the plan) just like anyone else. However, attorneys working on contract are subject to peculiar—and sometimes frustrating—limitations when it comes to other loan forgiveness programs.

Public Service Loan Forgiveness (PSLF)

As referenced in earlier chapters, the PSLF program allows eligible Direct loan borrowers to have any remaining federal student loan balance forgiven after 10 years of qualifying payments under an income-driven repayment plan, if the borrower works full time in public service. It's a great program for many borrowers. However, to qualify, the public service employer must certify that it *employs* the borrower in a full-time capacity. This can make some contractors ineligible for the PSLF program, even if they work in a public service capacity.

For instance, many states (and the federal government) supplement their public defender organizations with privately contracted attorneys. These attorneys, called "bar advocates" in some states, take on indigent criminal cases at a modest hourly rate set and paid by the state or federal government. Although these attorneys are indisputably doing important work for the public good, they are technically *private attorneys* who are being *contracted* by the government for legal services. These attorneys are paid directly by the government, but they are not *employees* of the government, in contrast to the people who work in public defender offices. Thus, bar advocates are unlikely to be eligible for the PSLF program.

Similarly, a private attorney who does contracted legal work for a nonprofit organization may not be considered to be in eligible PSLF employment if she is technically a private attorney, not an attorney *employed* by the nonprofit entity.

Loan Repayment and Assistance Programs (LRAPs)

Similarly, contract attorneys may be locked out of some law school LRAP programs. Eligibility for LRAP programs varies from law school to law school, but many schools require that their graduates be employed by a public interest/public service entity to qualify for an LRAP award. Attorneys working in private practice may not qualify, even if 100 percent of their work is public interest-oriented legal work under contract with public service entities. If you're a contract attorney performing public interest-related legal work, you should check the eligibility requirements of your law school and contact your financial aid office to determine whether or not you may qualify for an LRAP award.

16

Student Loan Management for the Non-Attorney

Not every person who graduates from law school becomes an attorney, and not every attorney practices law for their entire career. It is important to note that many of the student loan programs discussed in this book—income-driven repayment plans, Public Service Loan Forgiveness, deferment, and forbearance— are applicable to many federal student loan borrowers, regardless of their profession. Many of the loan repayment strategies described in Part 2 of this book may apply to other similarly situated professionals, even if they are not practicing law. You don't have to be a lawyer to effectively manage your student loan debt.

There are some student loan relief programs, however, that are specific to *other* career paths. Given the fact that many attorneys choose to leave the practice of law (even if only temporarily) at some point in their career, these programs are worth mentioning.

Teacher Loan Forgiveness

Teacher-based loan forgiveness allows up to **$17,500** of your federal student loans disbursed after October 1, 1998, to be canceled if all of these criteria are met:

- You teach for five consecutive years.
- As a full-time highly qualified math or science teacher, or as a special education teacher.
- In an eligible elementary or secondary school where a certain specified percentage of the students are low-income (to determine whether your school is an "eligible" low-income school, you can visit the U.S. Department of Education's school database, available at www.studentaid.ed.gov).

This forgiveness program is available to both Direct loan and FFEL loan borrowers. To be considered "highly qualified," the teacher must be certified as a teacher, must hold at least a bachelor's degree, and must be highly competent in the subject taught, as determined by the school and criteria set forth by the U.S.

Department of Education. If you are not a math, science, or special education teacher, there is a smaller $5,000 teacher loan forgiveness award that you can get if you work as a full-time highly qualified elementary school teacher for five consecutive years at an eligible school.

Most teachers are also eligible for the Public Service Loan Forgiveness program described earlier (provided they work in public or nonprofit private schools), but there's an important caveat: You cannot make progress toward Teacher Loan Forgiveness and Public Service Loan Forgiveness at the same time. Thus, for borrowers with federal loan balances that are substantially higher than the $17,500 Teacher Loan Forgiveness cap, it probably makes more sense to opt for the Public Service Loan Forgiveness program.

Perkins Loan Cancellation for Non-Attorneys

Public defenders and prosecuting attorneys aren't the only people who can get their Perkins loans canceled without paying a dime. In fact, Perkins loan cancellation is available for quite a few professions, including:

- Firefighters
- Nurses
- Medical technicians
- VISTA and Peace Corps volunteers
- Active duty military servicemembers working in a hostile area
- Certain librarians
- Employees of certain public or nonprofit child services or family services agencies providing assistance to low-income communities
- Certain people employed in the Head Start program
- Employees in a licensed prekindergarten or child care program
- Employees who provide certain services to people with disabilities
- Speech pathologists
- Special education teachers
- Math, science, and foreign language teachers
- Faculty members at a tribal college or university

This is indeed a motley crew of assorted professions that may qualify for Perkins loan cancellation, and some of the categories listed here may have even more specific requirements than just working in the designated profession. If you think you may be eligible for Perkins loan cancellation, the best first step would be to contact your school (the loan holder for Perkins loans) to determine your eligibility. You can then complete a Perkins loan cancellation application provided by the school or its designated third-party servicer.

Peace Corps and AmeriCorps

Volunteers serving in the Peace Corps and AmeriCorps have a number of federal student loan relief programs available to them. AmeriCorps members can get interest accrual waived on their federal student loans during their service, which essentially "freezes" their balance. Members must complete their service to qualify. Peace Corps volunteers can get most of their Perkins loans canceled if they complete their service. Both Peace Corps and AmeriCorps volunteers are eligible for special deferments or forbearances that allow them to postpone their payments during service periods with minimal penalties, and volunteers of both programs can also make progress toward Public Service Loan Forgiveness, either by making income-driven-based payments (which can be as low as $0/month) or by using the stipends provided by the program.

Military Servicemembers

There was a time when serving in the military could essentially guarantee a young American a free college education. Not anymore. Today, many people who serve in our armed forces are also student loan borrowers. Luckily, there are some important student loan benefits and programs that are specifically geared toward military servicemembers, although too few people are aware of them.

Caps on Interest Rates

The Servicemembers Civil Relief Act (SCRA) caps interest rates on all student loans (federal and private) at 6 percent for borrowers serving in "active duty" status. The U.S. Department of Education also halts all interest accumulation for up to five years for certain federal Direct loan borrowers who are serving in a "special pay" hostile area.

Military Deferment

Federal student loan borrowers serving in the military can defer payments on their loans during, and immediately following, certain active-duty deployments, such as a military operation or a national emergency. This is a deferment that you must affirmatively request and apply for.

Waiver of Documentation Requirements for Income-Based Repayment (IBR)

For obvious reasons, sending in annual documentation of income to recertify for income-driven repayment plans like IBR and PAYE might be difficult for borrowers actively serving in the military. The HEROES Act waives the annual recertification requirement for federal student loan borrowers in active-duty status, allowing them to extend their income-driven monthly payments beyond the typical 12-month period. You have to *request* the waiver, though—it is not automatic.

Public Service Loan Forgiveness

The military is a branch of the government and qualifies as a "public service" entity. Thus, full-time employees of the military may make progress toward Public Service Loan Forgiveness. Military servicemembers do not have to be in active-duty status to make progress toward this student loan forgiveness program; they simply must be working "full-time" for the military, even if it's in a civilian capacity.

Disability Discharge for Veterans

Veterans who have been certified as unable to work due to a service-connected disability may be eligible to have their federal student loans forgiven (although in this context it would technically be called a *discharge*). Certain private lenders also have disability discharge programs. These discharge programs often involve a rigorous application process, and the discharged balance may be treated as taxable income. Thus, it would be advisable to consult with an expert before applying.

17

The Future

The student loan landscape is changing, and the pace of reform is steadily quickening. During 2014 and 2015, the Obama administration proposed major changes to federal student loan repayment and forgiveness programs, including the expansion of income-driven repayment plan options through the Revised Pay As You Earn (REPAYE) plan, as well as the creation of new potential paths to loan forgiveness for certain borrowers defrauded by for-profit educational institutions. However, the administration has also called for other changes, such as modifications to the payment calculation for married borrowers, increases in student loan payments for higher-income earners, and even caps on the Public Service Loan Forgiveness program.

At the same time, members of Congress and other politicians have been proposing some of their own recipes to reform our massively complicated student loan system. Notable proposals include reintroducing bankruptcy protections for certain student loans; mandating income-driven repayment for *all* federal student loan borrowers and requiring direct payroll deductions for payments; creating new refinancing options that would allow federal student loan borrowers to lower their interest rates while keeping their loans in the federal system; and changing elements of the tax code to eliminate some tax deductions for student loan borrowers, while imposing additional taxes on certain federal student loan repayment and forgiveness programs.

What does this all mean? I think the breadth of these proposals is a clear indication that there is widespread and growing recognition that our student loan system is overly burdensome and complicated, especially for borrowers with high levels of debt and quite extreme variability in earning potential—like attorneys. The system has to be more efficient and easier to navigate, and it must provide more avenues of relief for borrowers who are being crushed by these debts.

Still, as I've highlighted throughout this book, despite the system's current flaws and shortcomings, the situation is not hopeless. There are programs and strategies available right now to borrowers in a variety of situations. If there's any takeaway from this little handbook, it's this: Know your situation, learn about these available programs and strategies, and use them. It can make a difference not only in your day-to-day life but also for your long-term future.

In the meantime, changes are coming. Some may be good for student loan borrowers, and some will be bad. Most likely, they will simply be imperfect. Some of the loan repayment and management options I've discussed in this book may be expanded, changed, restricted, or eliminated. New programs will likely be created in the coming years, and despite everyone's best intentions, these programs will have their own confusing array of eligibility criteria and caveats. I am hopeful that given the increasing national dialogue about the burdens of student loan debt, borrowers will ultimately benefit as lawmakers scrutinize the system.

Nevertheless, if you are a law student or an attorney trying to keep your head above water while you manage a huge student loan debt burden, along with one of the most volatile and stressful career tracks that you could have chosen (way to go!), *you can do this.* Use the resources and strategies I've described in this book to understand your student loan portfolio and the options available to you, and how best to integrate this into your life. If you still think you need some help, don't be afraid to seek it out: contact your loan servicer, talk to your school's financial aid office, or retain the services of a qualified professional who can help.

Ultimately, I am optimistic that we will see some positive reforms for student loan borrowers during the next several years.

I guess I'll just have to write a sequel.

Resources

Government Resources

- The federal student loan database (the "National Student Loan Data System") has key information about your current federal student loan holders: **www.nslds.ed.gov**
- The federal government's web portal for federal student loan management, where you can consolidate your federal student loans and select or renew income-driven repayment plans: **www.studentloans.gov**
- The federal government's web portal for accessing your free annual credit report, which you are entitled to under the Fair Credit Reporting Act and which may contain useful information about nonfederal student debts that you may have: **www.annualcreditreport.com**
- FedLoan Servicing, a subsidiary of the Pennsylvania Higher Education Assistance Association (PHEAA) and a contracted loan servicing company for the U.S. Department of Education, has several resources available for borrowers interested in Public Service Loan Forgiveness, including guidelines and access to important forms and applications. **www.myfedloan.org**

Nonprofit Resources

- The National Consumer Law Center has a significant amount of free information on student loans through its Student Loan Borrower Assistance Project: **www.nclc.org**
- The Project on Student Loan Debt, managed by The Institute for College Access and Success, maintains an informational resource for income-driven repayment plans and Public Service Loan Forgiveness, including repayment calculators and very helpful FAQ pages: **www.ibrinfo.org**
- The National Association of Consumer Advocates is an organization of consumer rights lawyers who only represent the interests of consumers and debtors. It has a directory on its website if you're looking for a lawyer: **www.consumeradvocates.org**
- FinAid.org is a nonprofit website containing a wealth of information about financial aid, repayment plans, and refinancing programs: **www.finaid.org**

Follow my blog, where I routinely write articles about student loans and the latest developments in higher education financing: **www.BostonStudentLoanLawyer.com**

Glossary

Acceleration: Condition in which the entire balance of the student loan becomes due immediately, usually when the borrower breaches the terms of the promissory note by failing to make required monthly installment payments. Acceleration typically occurs when a borrower is in default on a student loan.

Adjusted Gross Income (AGI): An individual's total gross income, minus certain specified allowances for personal exemptions and itemized deductions, as reported on the individual's U.S. tax return. AGI is typically used to calculate a borrower's monthly payment for federal income-driven repayment plans.

Administrative Forbearance: A special type of temporary forbearance for federal student loans that allows an individual to temporarily suspend monthly payments for a brief period (usually 30 to 90 days) while the borrower's application for income-driven repayment or consolidation is processed. This type of forbearance should not result in interest capitalization, unlike other forms of forbearance.

Alternative Documentation of Income: Any form of income documentation other than a tax return that can be used to calculate a borrower's monthly payment under a federal income-driven repayment plan. Examples include a pay stub or paycheck, a letter from an employer, a bank statement, copies of canceled checks, a profit-and-loss statement, or a self-certifying statement explaining in detail the source and frequency of income. Documentation should generally not be older than 90 days.

Auto-Debit: A program available for many student loans whereby student borrowers can set up automatic monthly payments through a debit/credit card or bank account. Some student loan servicers may offer a marginal interest rate reduction as an incentive to enter into auto-debit arrangements.

Bar Study Loan: A special type of private student loan that is available to law students after graduation to cover the costs of living expenses and preparatory courses during study for the bar exam.

Capitalization: The process by which outstanding interest that has accrued over a period of time is added to the loan principal balance.

Compounding: The process by which interest continues to accrue on a loan principal balance after interest capitalization has occurred. Compounding essentially results in interest accruing on interest. The combination of capitalization and compounding can lead to significant balance increases.

Consolidation: The process of combining several individual student loans, often held by different entities, into a single new student loan with one interest rate, one monthly payment, and one loan servicer. For federal student loan borrowers, the only federal consolidation program is the federal Direct consolidation loan program. There are also private student loan consolidation programs for both private and federal student loans.

Cosigner: An individual who signs a loan promissory note along with the student borrower, usually for a private student loan. The cosigner is typically fully and equally responsible for the entire cosigned student loan, just as the borrower is.

Default: Occurs when a borrower is in breach of the underlying student loan promissory note, often by failing to make monthly installment payments for a specified period of time (270 days for most federal student loans and usually 60 to 180 days for private student loans). Default typically results in the acceleration of the entire loan balance.

Deferment: An option for a student loan borrower to postpone monthly payments on a student loan for a specified reason, such as being in school or being unemployed. For certain federal student loans, the government may cover interest during deferment periods (in contrast to forbearance).

Delinquency: Occurs when a borrower falls behind on monthly installment payments. A period of delinquency usually precedes default and acceleration, and it sometimes can be cured.

Discretionary Income: For purposes of calculating a borrower's monthly payment under federal income-driven repayment plans, discretionary income is the difference between the borrower's adjusted gross income and 150 percent of the poverty guideline for the borrower's family size. Discretionary income does not factor in a borrower's living expenses.

Federal Direct Loans: Federal student loans that are issued directly by the U.S. Department of Education. Since the discontinuation of the FFEL program in 2010, most new federal student loans are issued through the Direct loan program.

Federal Family Education Loan (FFEL) Program: A federal student lending program whereby student loans were issued by private lenders, which were in turn insured by guaranty agencies, and ultimately backed by—and assignable to—the federal government. The FFEL program was discontinued in 2010.

Fixed Rate: A student loan interest rate that stays the same during the loan's repayment term.

Forbearance: An option for a student loan borrower to postpone monthly payments on a student loan for a specified reason, such as an economic or medical hardship. Interest continues to accrue on federal and private student loans during periods of forbearance and may be periodically capitalized.

Grace Period: A one-time-use period, following graduation or exit from an in-school deferment, during which no payments are due on a student loan but interest continues to accrue.

Guaranty Agency: A state-created agency or nonprofit organization that is part of the Federal Family Education Loan (FFEL) program. The guaranty agency "insures" a FFEL loan for the original lender and will take over the loan from the lender if the student borrower defaults. The guaranty agency can ultimately assign the defaulted student loan to the U.S. Department of Education if it cannot collect on the loan.

Income-Driven Repayment: A repayment plan that uses a formula to calculate a unique monthly payment for a borrower based on the borrower's income and family size. There are several income-driven repayment plans, each with its own unique formulas and eligibility criteria. These plans are typically available only to federal student loan borrowers.

Interest: Money charged on a student loan as a percentage of the loan principal. Interest rates may be fixed or variable, and accrued interest (if unpaid) may be periodically capitalized, depending on the terms of the loan promissory note.

Loan Repayment Assistance Programs (LRAPs): Programs financed by law schools that provide law graduates with stipends, grants, or convertible loans to help defray the costs of student loan repayment.

Loan Servicer: The entity that handles the day-to-day operations of a non-defaulted student loan, including billing and payment processing, repayment plan selection, and eligibility determinations for various programs such as deferments and forbearance.

Negative Amortization: The process whereby a student loan balance increases even while the borrower pays the minimum required monthly payments because the monthly payment is less than the amount of monthly interest that accrues on the loan principal. This may occur under federal income-driven repayment plans.

Origination Fee: A fee charged by a student loan lender (federal or private) when the borrower enters into a loan agreement with the lender. The origination fee becomes part of the loan principal balance that the borrower must repay.

Principal: The original disbursed balance of a student loan. The principal balance may decrease over time as the borrower makes payments, or may increase due to interest capitalization.

Private Student Loan: A student loan for which the lender is an entity *other than* the federal government, and the loan is not backed or guaranteed by the federal government through the Federal Family Education Loan (FFEL) program.

Promissory Note: The signed student loan contract between the borrower and the lender that establishes the borrower's obligation to repay the loan under specified terms and conditions.

Public Service Loan Forgiveness (PSLF): A federal student loan program that allows any remaining federal student loan balance to be forgiven after the borrower has made 120 qualifying monthly payments under specified repayment plans while working full time for a qualifying public service employer.

Refinancing: Modifying an existing student loan, or taking out a new student loan, to obtain a lower interest rate or more favorable loan repayment terms.

Rehabilitation: A program whereby a borrower in default on a federal student loan can restore the loan to good standing through a temporary repayment arrangement based on the borrower's income or total financial circumstances.

Settlement: An agreement between a lender and a borrower to compromise on a defaulted student loan and allow the borrower to make a payment for less than the full amount due, usually in a lump sum, in exchange for a waiver of the remaining balance.

Variable Rate: An interest rate that changes over the course of the student loan's repayment term. Variable rates are sometimes, but not always, capped.

About the Author

Adam S. Minsky is one of the nation's leading experts on student debt and is a pioneer in his field. He established the first law firm in Massachusetts devoted entirely to assisting student loan borrowers, and he remains one of the only attorneys in the country with a practice focused exclusively in this field of law. Attorney Minsky has published numerous books and articles on student debt, and he regularly speaks at colleges, nonprofit organizations, and professional associations about developments in student loan law and higher education financing. Major media outlets frequently seek his expert opinions on national news and policy stories. Attorney Minsky was named a Massachusetts Super Lawyer "Rising Star" for 2015.

Attorney Minsky founded his student loan law practice because he took out student loans to help finance his own education, but when he encountered a serious problem with one of his student loan servicers, he couldn't find anyone to help him. He started his firm to help other borrowers who feel alone and overwhelmed by a student debt issue, and he has helped hundreds of clients work through major problems with their student loans.

Attorney Minsky received his undergraduate degree, with honors, from Boston University and his law degree from Northeastern University School of Law. He continues to call the Boston area home.

Index